SUFFOLK
COUNTRY
SCHOOLDAYS

H. Mills West

Illustrations by Stephen J. Govier

COUNTRYSIDE BOOKS
NEWBURY, BERKSHIRE

First published 1995
© H. Mills West 1995

COUNTRYSIDE BOOKS
3 Catherine Road
Newbury, Berkshire

ISBN 1 85306 343 6

Designed by Mon Mohan
Illustrations by Stephen J. Govier

Produced through MRM Associates Ltd., Reading
Typeset by Paragon Typesetters, Queensferry, Clwyd
Printed by J.W. Arrowsmith Ltd., Bristol

Contents

Author's Note: The village called Hempston is a composite name for several real villages in Suffolk, upon which the events related in this book are based.

1

1875 – THE SMALL PIONEERS

- Stephen J Govier 1995 -

THE village school opened in my native village of Hempston in the year 1875. Just before the fateful day someone threw a stone during the dark hours of the night and broke a window. It was one of the big windows at the playground end and high up. When the pupils began to arrive there was the jagged star-shaped hole gaping in the morning light as a lesser mystery in the immense perplexity of school life that was looming before them. The broken window was the only protest of a violent kind in the village and a brand-new headmistress with a brand-new broom soon whisked the debris out of sight. Beneath the surface, I believe, there was a good deal of resentment among the cottagers but they knew better than to show open hostility to the judgment of their betters.

That morning children came to school for the first time by law. They came from all over the village as far as the Green and the lonely turnpike house, and a whole crowd of unwilling gnomes dragged along from the populous Row. Most of the children arrived in family or neighbourly groups, holding hands some of them as if to share their fears as to where their hesitant steps were leading them. Others were alone; some walked defiantly along, kicking the dust with their toe-gaping boots and swearing like seasoned farm-men; and some were solitary innocents who seemed scarcely to have discovered the light of day.

They all came out of the quiet morning, largely unattended by adults and generally afraid. Once they reached the pound which was to be their playground they waited stiffly together, the faces of friends and strangers alike drained of all but misery. It was a day that was to pass with deadly slowness, one they would remember for the rest of their lives. Little consolation it would have given them to know that they were pioneers in a great social and educational venture.

Nevertheless, these were the first of the 'scholars' – for, though not many of them were over ten years old and most had never yet seen the inside of a school, they were designated 'scholars' in the phraseology of the day. Two of the first scholars on that long ago day were my own aunt and uncle, the eldest children of my grandparents who had married in 1866, just four years before that fateful Act instituting compulsory schooling.

*   *   *   *   *   *

My grandfather I only knew when he was a very old man with a white beard and severe black clothes but in his time he had been a village character idolised for his physical strength and high spirits. A rare good man, the farmers agreed, and the women, young mawthers and matrons alike, said silently 'Amen'. In 1866 Grandfather could have taken his pick from the servant girls for miles around and was not unknown as a nocturnal visitor to the daughters of farmers nearby, but there was never any doubt in his mind as to who he was going to marry. From the beginning his heart was set on Eliza – Eliza Peck from the same village and employed at the very same farm where Grandfather worked. Together at Oakenfield Farm, with 400 acres under the plough in those days, they formed bonds of close association that carried them undeviatingly through their long life together.

By that time Grandfather had risen quickly through the considerable hierarchy of Oakenfield farm workers and at 25 years old was second to the head horseman. As for Eliza, she had a place of considerable respect in the farmhouse as house-parlourmaid. During the harvest that year she would often slip away from the domestic duties and hurry down to the fields in the modest black dress that was her afternoon uniform. She watched as he worked or made bands of straw for the tying of sheaves. Afterwards, when all the carting was done, she bent regularly in the fields for the gleaning. They worked together on the same farm, within sight sometimes, within the familiar orbit of field and farmhouse and village – and the long days of toil demanded of them they accepted as a rightful burden and an earnest of harder days that would come when they married.

After the harvest was over and the tumbrils began to cart the manure out from the yards, they came together to the church and kneeled in stiff, Sunday clothes before the altar and were blessed. For fun that day, Grandfather had put a miniature whip in the lapel of his coat. It was the sign of his calling and he had worn this very one at the hiring fair years before when he had first been engaged to work at Oakenfield. The little quirk of humour made the day for there was not the dullest wit but who could slyly eye the bride and the whip and find a quip or a question that would make for a side-splitting guffaw among the male guests. After the ceremony in the church everyone followed the pair on foot in a little untidy procession down the sandy lane to the cottage. Behind them came the children, stumbling in the excitement of wearing their best clothes, skipping over the loose stones and over the hoof-marks of farm horses scored deep in the sand.

It was a day that no one now living remembers and I must reach back to my own youth to recall how others spoke of it. Enough, now, to believe that it was of unclouded happiness for Eliza and George – that day and, I hope, many a day to come. After all, the golden age of farming still flourished and workers shared in the prosperity of good corn prices and enjoyed a comfortable security in their jobs. All seemed well with the world, in such small compass as they knew it. Even if they had known, as they walked with friends and neighbours down the quiet lanes that the clouds were already gathering it would have diminished nothing.

In the very same month that Eliza and George were married, an official appeared in the village in connection with a national head-counting of potential schoolchildren. As he proceeded with his task under the gaze of the cottage windows, he must have appeared, in his citified clothes and fussy manner, to be the very personification of interfering bureaucracy. It was said that, a few miles away, he had been rough-handled, his hat thrown into a pond and the dogs let loose at cottage doors. Here, in Hempston, his canvassing was observed from curtained windows with acute suspicion, though most people understood that this was merely some jack-in-office under orders. It was not until the man reached the Row that things began to look ugly, for here he was jostled from house to house in a very rough fashion and he was forced to obtain much of his information from the village gossips.

There was cause enough to distrust and dread the threat of enforced schooling. Experience through generation after generation had taught country people to depend upon themselves. For the basic needs of filling their stomachs and covering backs the families of agricultural labourers had to work together, to hunt and forage for the domestic good. Authority, they knew, would do precious little for them in that direction and they intended to do precious little for authority. All they asked was the right to fight and survive by their own efforts. To some it was a thought intolerable that distant officials planned to interfere with their lives and add another burden. In the Row, where the rough families lived in close-built hovels, there was a simmering of violence and hate against all those in power. In the safety of their own walls they railed against the government and the school boards and all those who dealt in book-learning. As for the Squire and the Lord above, they might have complained about these too except that it was known that both had notoriously long ears.

When the Act became law it was from the Row – and similar village hovels all over the country – that the toughest of the first scholars came. They were hoarse-voiced and hard-bitten from poverty and ignorance. Some looked grimed and wizened little old men, others were dull, coarse and un-kempt. They spat, swore and fought among themselves, revealed their nakedness to the girls and extorted homage from the meek. In the classroom, where they found them-selves to be at a disadvantage, they sulked and kept their own counsel. For them it was a fiercely unhappy mobilisation. Not only were they robbed of freedom but in the glare of school life their weaknesses and poverty were shown, ring-worm, flea-bites and rags for all to see. Some, indeed, brought by the hand even poorer creatures who would have spent their lives in a domestic twilight, who had physical disabilities or were sick or vacant of mind. The school bell rang for all until it became expedient, as well as humanitarian, to exempt a few. To many who heard it, the bell must have seemed oppressive and the life to which it called the scholars a senseless punishment.

Even to those families more amenable to change, the value

of education for the traditional employments of the village seemed doubtful. With few exceptions boys went to work on the farms nearby as soon as they were big enough to be of any use and in the natural course of things became expert stockmen or shepherds, ploughmen or carters. Never had they needed book-learning to satisfy a farmer – there were other priorities. Willingness, 'sharpness' and physical strength would qualify for a place anywhere. Boys with those qualities in some degree or other flocked to join the considerable numbers of men who, in those days, worked on farms of moderate size. On Oakenfield itself there were 23 men to deal with 400 acres and it was a matter of frequent calculation that there were even more on Brick-kiln Farm and Pightle.

Sixteen fine horses were worked at Oakenfield and these were the great attraction for small boys setting out on their first job. Invariably they would plump to work with the horses, and the foreman, with more good humour than was shown by most of his kind, would tell them 'Sune as yew c'n harness a hoss yew c'n take an' work it'. There was no mistake among country boys as to what this entailed but there were always a few who were determined enough to take up the challenge. Farm workers could always tell stories of small figures arriving in the morning half-light to stand in the manger of some great shire or Suffolk horse and stretch and struggle to get the heavy collar on. It was the collar that beat them and allowed the foreman to point out that there was a good deal to be said for looking after smaller animals like pigs and sheep.

One thing was certain: if boys could manage without book-learning then it was a sheer waste of time and money for girls. What on earth would they use it for? To write a note to a lover one day, perhaps, to sign their real names in the church register when they got married, to read laboriously out of the Bible on dull, long Sundays? It was a doubtful kind of acquisition at best.

In 'service', as on the farms, jobs were plentiful because the labour was cheap. At Hempston Rectory there were five servants in a simple hierarchy headed by the cook, all of them busy and apparently contented on their side of the green baize door. At the Manor it was a much grander extent of servitude, with footman and butler as well as a host of females. Each of the farmhouses, too, had its modicum of domestic help. A new young girl could be slipped into the menage of such households and scarcely be noticed. The fact that she would receive almost nothing in wages for a year or two was of little account. Her parents would be satisfied that she had a 'situation' and would be given food and lodging and an appropriate uniform in a respectable house. It was a proper place for a girl to be.

In these long-established concepts of village life it was natural that schooling should seem to be an unnecessary luxury. The Act was awaited with grumbling concern as to the sanity of city folk and their motives in undermining the old order of family life. When at last the law was passed, the sharpness of change was muted by the time-lag of effective implementation. Few of the more slippery kind of scholars could be caught immediately in the net and for the whole operation a margin of ten years was allowed. In that time older children could escape the meshes if they wriggled enough. At the same time younger ones would gradually become accustomed to the prospect. Once the pioneers had opened the way the tradition of school attendance had begun and made its influence felt.

In any case, not all of the first compulsory scholars were toughs, by any means. Some came to surrender themselves with good grace, their parents seeing in school life a civilising influence and a means by which their offspring could better themselves. In fact, a good proportion of the more amenable scholars already attended school voluntarily. In Hempston, before the Act provided a school for the village, a round dozen boys had walked to the British School at Barkham, while the longer four-mile journey to Binham where there was a National School was taken by three sons of a small farmer. Each morning the farmer drove them to school in his dogcart, but in the afternoon, when the farm milking had to take precedence, the three boys had to trudge back on their own lagging feet.

What these voluntary pupils learned did not amount to a great deal outside the scriptures: it was a weakness of the system that voluntary interest was short-lived and an average spell of schooling was about two years. However, it seemed a good thing for respectable families to do at a time when the ethic of Samuel Smiles and self-improvement was gaining ground in rural areas. Of necessity in the Victorian village, aspiration was of a limited and personal kind. Few would have dared to see education as a possible challenge to class difference or as a step towards social advancement. The traditional distinctions of society were too firmly implanted in rich and poor alike to permit such ideas.

Already the dangers of a rude peasantry being able to read and write were clearly seen by the privileged classes – doubts about the wisdom of conferring literacy upon all and sundry were voiced by those who were already literate. Such fears, arising from some of the most influential people in the land, were mollified by the frequent assurances of the educational reformers that the schooling to be offered to the masses would be limited to the most basic achievements except in the sphere of spiritual doctrine. 'One of the most important lessons,' proclaimed the National Schools Committee, 'will be the duty of resignation to their lot. By the very constitution of Society the Poor are destined to labour and to this supreme and beneficial arrangement of Providence they must of necessity submit.'

At that time in Hempston there used to be six privies that stood like sentry boxes along the ditch behind the ten houses of the Row. In the front where the tiny areas designated as gardens touched the road there were two water pumps. This odd apportionment of basic facilities was often debated by the more respectable villagers and a superior note was often sounded by the question – how ever did the families in the

Row manage to raise their such abundant progeny in such poky little houses? The Row swarmed with children, in doorways and back yards, in mailcarts and soap-boxes, indoors and out, until that blessed day arrived when each could venture further afield and earn a minute contribution to the board. At eight or nine years the boys became too old to play, setting their immediate sights on simple, time-dragging occupations like bird-scaring or keeping an eye on pigs or sheep. For a long week spent on such tasks in the open field a wage of sixpence was little enough reward but a necessary part of the weekly budget at home.

Besides that, it was essential apprenticeship for a country boy. At his solitary task he would learn a good deal about the world that was never told in books and furthermore learn with a real and pressing motive – to use his wits and knowledge to help salve the perennial poverty that he shared with his family. To this end, he developed a canny shrewdness and the proudest thing that a cottager could say of his growing son was that he was a 'regular sharper'. At the same time, the boy developed the kind of patience he needed to understand the ways of nature and how to use them for his own profit. So he learned to make snares for rabbits and to set them in just the right places, to kill a rabbit quickly and quietly with a sharp blow behind the head, to skin it and dry the pelt in the sun. He soon knew how to use a ferret, how to trap sparrows and bullfinches, decoy pigeons and even how to snatch a sleeping pheasant from a branch. His life was lightened by the endless consideration of the wiles and tricks of a hunter, which had to include the clandestine ways of the poacher, a perilous role for anyone in those days.

Equally important was to discover the 'lie of the land' in his relationships with other people. From hard experience he learned to 'keep in' with the farm cowman while also keeping out of range of the farmer's boot. He knew to whom it was politic to touch his forelock and who would be likely to give him a couple of swedes in return for an odd job. For a boy in this environment the priorities he recognised were simple and unchanging – food for today and if possible for tomorrow; boots, clothing for the basic purpose of keeping warm; enough savings eventually to be buried properly without the smear of pauperism. If luxuries were ever considered, then a watch and chain or a walking-stick with a silver band, perhaps a music-box or a brass-bound Bible were things to dream about.

I have known and worked with such boys when they had grown into old men. They were called out in their dotage from their chimney seats and carried off to work in the sugarbeet fields by the food demands of the Second World War. But now they were anachronisms, for life had changed about them and they were still bound to the ancient wisdom of the fields learned long ago. Working with these men on the land they knew so intimately was to realise that in their lonely childhood the field and the wood had been all things to them – their natural school from choice and inheritance. In a way the old men were the true custodians of the land. They could tell the whole genealogy of farm ownership for miles around, they remembered ancient field names and forgotten footpaths and they would speak of the characters and fates of farm horses perhaps 40 years dead. Deeper still, in their own idiom and with no knowledge of agricultural science, they talked of the soil and the miracle of growth. All of it in the slow, rich phrases of old East Anglia and for no one to hear but themselves. All of it remembered as something important though the rest of the world had become a perplexity. Even now, in the midst of war, the old men read no newspapers and had no patience for the radio and the words they heard from others of battles and events they had little faith in. Long ago they had learned to depend on no one but themselves and to distrust whatever was outside their experience. The old men knew they were anachronisms and they kept their own reality to themselves, knowing the earth in a way that no one would ever again need to know.

When such as these were children and the threat of compulsory schooling was becoming a reality, there were other

problems that faced them besides their own poverty and ignorance. Often, for example, they would be caught in a miserable situation between the demands of the school and the natural resentment in their own homes. Many a one, given a task of reading by a teacher, would try and make out the words as he sat on the cottage step or on his stool beside the kitchen fire and incur the indignation of his parents at such an unnatural practice. My grandmother, she who had come to the church as a bride that autumn day in 1866, used to make it quite clear when she was an old lady what she thought of books and book-readers. 'You'll tarn yar head properly silly reading them owd books,' she would often say.

It was the apparent passivity – the sitting down or lounging that accompanied reading – that vexed her. It looked like laziness, a kind of negative occupation when a boy should be doing things. It was unnatural, she thought. In that house, as in many another, the whole weight of domestic troubles and frustrations could be turned in anger against an early scholar for apparently betraying the real nature of cottage life. He was the cause, however unwillingly, of depriving the family of money spent on the school fees and of his potential earnings; he was the root of their disappointment at having lost a 'sharper' and gained a fool. Worst of all, perhaps, he would get all sorts of ideas into his head that would lead him to think he was superior. 'Too big for his boots,' cottagers would opine when some young member of the family tried to advance some piece of knowledge he had learned at school.

Perhaps the real cause of these attitudes lay in the lack of school tradition. There were no precedents to use as a guide and the way for beginners was hard and completely unknown. To be one of the first to be captured and made to sit through the long daylight hours in a walled-up classroom was often unbearable, impossible. The immediate, overwhelming need for many an untamed young scholar was to escape, never mind the probable consequences of a beating at school and another at home following the visit from the

School Board man. Come what may, many ran away from the school in the early days; some, in fear of the School Board man, fled from home and school together.

A village school logbook records: 'Two children endeavoured to play truant this week: one succeeded but the other was captured and brought back to school struggling violently for liberty.' It is difficult not to be persuaded by the language in which this episode is described that the school must have been regarded as a veritable prison. The punishment given to the 'two children' (inconceivably girls!) is not recorded: to the timid and to those who found that booklearning came easily, the lesson was clear. But for the minority to whom captivity in school was unendurable there was no punishment that could hold them. For a time the determined truant kept authority at bay. Then the special Truant Schools were built whose treatment was harsh and punitive and whose dreadful reputation filtered through to every school in the land.

One of those who made a break for freedom in the early days of the new school at Hempston was my uncle Frank, in conspiracy with young Charlie Mayhew from the Glebe Cottages. Uncle Frank was the second of my grandparents' six sons and, to do him justice, was by no means the kind of rebel that the episode might show him to be. In fact, he became a ready scholar when he grew used to the idea and won many prizes for such things as memorising a whole chapter of the Bible and writing the Apostles' Creed in beautiful letters, feats that seemed to give the early educationists immense satisfaction. But Uncle Frank, like many others, had to be broken in to the new life. It was after only a week of incarceration that by the light of a cold and inauspicious autumn morning he and Charlie secured their few worldly possessions in the bottom of a meal sack and set out into the waiting world. The adventure, alas, was brief and little was seen of the promised land of freedom before they were spotted at the river side by some nosey-parker who alerted the School Board man. Luckily, the river at that point was neither wide nor deep, for Frank, who had been paddling, leapt back further into the water when he spied the enemy approaching. In a mad panic he waded through waterweed and squelching mud until the water was up to his waist. Then, in mid-stream he turned again, afraid to go further, afraid of running away without Charlie, afraid of going home wet through, afraid of the School Board man. He stood and sobbed at the certainty that it was a very unkind and unhappy world.

2

THE SCHOOL INSPECTOR

Stephen J. Govier - 1995-

THE way of the schoolboy has always been hard – and never so hard as at the beginning of compulsory schooling. Not only did he have to confront, for the first time and without a boy's natural weapons, the frightening presence of scholarship, but scholarship itself seemed to have little idea what kind of animal it was dealing with. The only certainty was that the scholar would experience all the spiritual benefits conferred by the utmost stringency of control. Even the more progressive educationists agreed that a little parsimony was a good thing for keeping youngsters in their places. Others thought the whole thing to be a wicked waste and a piece of misguided philanthropy.

The authoritative guide to the new project lay in the findings of the Newcastle Commission, whose deliberations had been made some years before. The Commission's lodestone was economy and the inquiry that it made into the conditions of existing voluntary schools and the future of compulsory schools left no doubt that such national beneficence as was proposed would be provided in a way that no cringing child or harassed teacher would be allowed to forget. In the new schools, it was proposed, there would be seven graded standards of attainment and each scholar would be required to pass into a new standard each year by strict examination in order to qualify for his small part of the school grant. In addition, he would have to make a minimum number of attendances.

These were twin fetters whose weight lay immediately upon the teacher who, with his salary and reputation at stake, had to transfer them to the unwilling scholar. If the School Board demanded this or that of Standard Five then Standard Five would learn it, willy-nilly, with or without the persuasion of the stick. In the same way, a child who looked like failing to make the requisite number of attendances would get a good deal of verbal and, if necessary, physical assistance to attend school and get his mark.

'Payment by Results', the system came to be called. Its only redeeming feature was that it sought to shake out the occasional inefficient school and slothful teacher. But the main and lasting effect was to ossify the brave new learning into the basic requirements of each of the seven standards, creating a rigid course of scholarship and harsh treatment to ensure that it was done. In addition to the set standards of the three Rs a great deal of attention had to be given to scriptural knowledge, not only to satisfy the original educational bodies of the Church but also because it was the general feeling of the times that a scholar would benefit by a degree of dressing-down by God as well as by the teacher.

So, through all the strata of those concerned in the system

– the taxpayer, the Department, the Inspectorate and the teacher – the pressure came down finally upon the schoolchild. It came down heavily upon his unwilling shoulders in the form of hard, monotonous work and unsympathetic treatment, of uncomfortable, cheap benches and inadequate books and massive, undigested religious dogma. On any one day in the year the total misery was enough but there was one day when the whole of the crushing weight of scholarship crystallised into the person of the Inspector on his annual visit.

At Hempston such visits usually took place in early August, perhaps immediately before the harvest holidays, and on that day, no matter what prayers may have been offered up for his delay, the Inspector would arrive bright and early and armed already with lists and standards. Often enough he would come by horse and trap from some convenient hotel in the district and if he were a considerate man who had breakfasted and slept well, all might go right enough during the day. If, as it seems by the records of such visits to have been more likely, he were dictatorial and egocentric or had derived little pleasure either from his lodging or from his open-air drive, then the day would be lost even before it began.

It was such a hard-fisted zealot who came to Hempston at the end of the first year of the new school and again in the second and third year. His visits came to be more dreaded than those of mad old Mrs Hawkes from the Row who came regularly to the school with the avowed intention of thrashing the teacher. His name was Redfield and he had the very conscious distinction of being an MA of Oxford. It was his duty, he felt, not only to demonstrate how little the village scholars had learned but also how little they were likely to get by way of grant. Mr Redfield was a fitting emissary of his erudite, cheese-paring masters for he carried the blighting message into the schools as a crusade.

The first skirmish of the day began with a critical examination of the short list of names which the head teacher would put before him as qualifying for exemption from examination for one reason or another. By the regulations a few children might be excused on special grounds and it would be in the head teacher's interest to make the list as long as possible, while the Inspector would be equally concerned to reduce the numbers. The hard bargaining was only part of the manoeuvring over the grant. Another ploy was for the teacher to keep children in lower standards where they would probably pass the examination rather than in higher ones where they might fail. The Inspector, on his part, could pursue his examination in such a way that children could not possibly understand, least of all the slow-thinking scholars of Hempston. Mr Redfield's manner alone was enough to frighten them out of their wits. They were dumb before him as he demanded erudite answers to pedantic questions, dumb and rigid with anxiety and apprehension. Failure to satisfy the Inspector would bring the wrath of the teacher upon their heads.

So the long agony of the day wore on. In his worse moods Mr Redfield would set out deliberately to humiliate and confuse the luckless examinees and when all were thoroughly demoralised he would turn his august attention to the near-sacred register. No matter that it had already been checked half a dozen times by conscientious school governors, the register, because of its importance in the yielding of the grant, would be subjected to the most searching scrutiny and alterations seized upon as a hint of possible false entries. Eventually, even he had to agree that a certain number of children seemed to have made the requisite attendances. The teacher would then seek to soften the Inspector's attitude by showing him the darning or stitching that the Rector's wife was teaching the girls. A finished sampler might be brought to his attention that embodied the words of a scriptural text and which expressed nothing more clearly than that it had been worked at for an unconscionable long time by fingers that might have been happier doing other things. At the end, when scholar and teacher alike were limp with nerves, they would raise shaky voices to sing a hymn or an appropriate folk song, for singing was one of the first permitted departures from the confines of the three Rs and could earn a grant for the school of a shilling a head.

Sometimes, desperation raised the dour contest to a new and memorable level. In the second year's examination Mr Redfield had young Percy Bower before him and was making a great to-do about the pronunciation of a certain word. Poor Percy stood dumbly, sinking from sheer fright into a native, sullen defiance. As the hated voice went on and on, Percy raised one threatening foot and glowered at the Inspectorial waistcoat button nearest to him until the limit came and the boot shot forward with the viciousness of panic. It brought a sharp 'Oh!' from the enemy as the boot landed on his shin but the exclamation was almost unnoticed as Percy made his own verbal contribution to the situation. In this desperate moment of release he turned back from the obtuse world of learning to the commonsense of family and field. 'You silly owd bugger,' he shouted. Then, as if to emphasise that his actions were by no means to be construed as friendly, he spat towards the majestic expanse of waistcoat and was off like an eel past the hands that tried to detain him. In the shocked silence of the school Percy could be heard scooting over the loose gravel of the playground. As he passed the windows he shouted: 'You wait – I'll kill you,' but he was sobbing, knowing that in the end he could not win.

From this time on, Percy was to have a largely undeserved reputation in the village as a rebel and a scamp. Respectable families noted him as one with whom their children should not associate. The truth was that his wrong-doings, as on the day of the inspection, were hardly ever more than efforts arising from a need to extricate himself from an untenable situation. Basically, he would not hurt a fly, but when his slow comprehension placed him in a spot where he felt he was being taken advantage of, his peasant sullenness rose and choked him. He had to fight to free himself.

On that day long ago there was a brief but precious spell

of liberty for Percy and a lightening of young hearts still imprisoned in the school. There was little triumph to be gained, however, for authority always had the last word. Where authority was represented by Mr Redfield the last word could be damning. By the time Percy had reached the shelter of the farm buildings near his home, the Inspector had finished the totalling of lists and standards and called portentously for the school logbook. In it he wrote in his great sprawling hand as intimidating as the message itself: 'Far from satisfactory. The grant is reduced by one-tenth for faults in instruction and writing and arithmetic. Discipline is wanting.'

For the head teacher standing by, such a report was often the final ignominy of a year's joyless struggle. Usually the comment was merely derogatory but could be scathing and even insulting. Worst of all the words were inscribed for all posterity to see. If, as happened here at Hempston, the Inspector took a personal dislike to the school, the inmates could expect no mercy. At the end of the following year a comment even more terse and bitter appears in the logbook: 'Arithmetic poor, dictation inaccurate, grammar feeble.' It was followed by a postscript threatening to invoke the near-divine powers of his masters. 'My Lords will expect better results next year.'

The phrase became a familiar parting blow in the area of Mr Redfield's administration. Whether it was intended to warn or to intimidate or whether, like many another sycophant he derived some pleasure from the remotest of associations with superior powers, it is difficult to say. The shadows of their Lordships followed Mr Redfield from village to village until the threat lost its impact and teachers told themselves that in any case their noble displeasure was hardly likely to be worse than the Inspector's.

Three days after witnessing a similar comment in her logbook, a schoolmistress of a village school not three miles from Hempston wrote her resignation immediately underneath, as well as that of her pupil teacher. It was almost the

last entry. During the four years of the school the book had recorded all the events, the punishments, triumphs and disappointments − first of all in a bright, flourishing style that was full of optimism and then declining to little more than a scribble that noted only necessary facts. Then there was the notice of resignation under the Inspector's report and nothing else − except for the last little note, somehow sadly out of sequence, 'There is no more sewing material'.

The next headmistress at the same school was made of sterner stuff. She took the war into the enemy's camp by capping the Inspector's (not Mr Redfield) comparatively mild comment with an acid comment of her own. 'Mr. A.,' she wrote underneath in the logbook, 'actually seemed disappointed at the general intelligence of the children and no credit was given to the teachers for a year of very hard work.'

As time went on and a more liberal attitude gradually lightened the gloom of the three Rs, so also softened the old hostilities. New concessions were allowed, new subjects introduced – and in 1890 the system of payment by results came to an end.

In those early days of general schooling there could have been no one with less interest in the clamour about education than my grandfather. Both he and Grandmother could write their names, if need be, which was hardly ever, and both followed the belief that filling a child's head with ideas was not the best way to prepare him for a simple country life. If there had been any way of opting out of the scheme I am sure both Grandfather and Grandmother would have been happy and relieved to take it but there was no alternative. As it happened, the time of their wedding and the starting of a family coincided so closely with the coming of the school that, unwilling though they were to take any pleasure in the matter, they came to know through their growing brood of children the whole gamut of early schooling experience and it is on this, retold to me or overheard in my young days, that I am now drawing.

The first two of their children, as I mentioned, were caught in the net on the very first day. They were my aunt and uncle – Ellen and Henry. Ellen, the first-born, was fair, taller than most ten-year-olds, gravely serious and always 'as good as gold'. She was one of those elder daughters who were destined, in those days, to become a secondary mother to younger ones as successive members of the family arrived. Yet she was also the most outward-looking of the whole family, happy to make friends and afraid of no one. When the lean years came, it was Ellen who suffered most, both from privation at home and humiliation in the village.

Henry, only a year younger, was by nature and his own cheerful acceptance, a country bumpkin. He had no doubts about his role and was only disturbed by other people's efforts to prove that he 'could do better'. At school the opinion was backed by some physical persuasion to make more effort and there is no doubt that such measures had spectacular results. A beating would be followed by a flash of real achievement as brilliant as it was short-lived. It is possible to plot the whole of Henry's school career as a series of cane-produced peaks of scholarship between the long levels of mere contentment. The stinging pain on his hands or buttocks made him swift to learn and gabble vast chunks of the Bible or to fashion letters in incomparable copper-plate – but it made no difference to him in the end. It was Ellen only who could influence him. With the rest of the brood who followed he looked up to her with respect for her judgment and authority. They clung to her, young as she was, meekly and trustingly through the daily routines of rising, dressing and preparing for school – and all day long they were aware of her comforting presence in the higher standard on the other side of the wooden screen.

Every Monday morning Ellen carried the school fees – first for just the two of them then later for as many as five, as they made their foot-dragging procession from the cottage to the school. At the beginning the weekly fee was a penny for each child but at the worst possible moment for the family the amount was doubled, though there was a concession if more than three from one family attended. To balance such generosity the fees for farmers' children were set at sixpence. It was something that no one felt happy about – parents took it as deliberately unjust, with some reason, that they were not only compelled to send their children to school but to use their hard-earned pennies to pay for the privilege. To teachers the school pence added a considerable burden beyond the simple bounds of book-keeping.

Children would turn up at school on Monday morning without their pennies. What should the head teacher do? It was a vexing problem in a system where both the fees and a minimum attendance were required. To send children home again when their mark was desperately needed on the register seemed wasteful and unwise. On the other hand, if it became known that children were allowed to stay without having paid the fees, it would provide a precedent for every opportunist family in the village. At Hempston, the headmistress dealt with the problem as best she could, to the extent of working out a system whereby dockets issued to pupils would at least establish whether or not the missing fees were lost or deliberately withheld. As far as she dared, she accepted promises instead of cash from families known to be honest, while the backsliders of the village were kept aware of their responsibilities by a barrage of threats and appeals.

It was all with very little effect. As the arrears of certain families mounted, the Rector was brought in to add his weight in the form of a strongly-worded talk to the whole school. The response was good – but temporary. In another few weeks the headmistress had to make the troubling decision that in future there could be no exceptions to prompt payment and anyone who came to school without their fees must be sent home again. So it happened that, time after time, families of small scholars were compelled to trudge back to their homes the way they had come. When this happened, they seldom reappeared the same day or even in the same week.

Every morning and afternoon at the beginning of lessons the register lay upon the teacher's desk as if it were a holy thing, but it was kept there by no comfortable religion. There were few days when it was not something to worry over, when the quota of scholars present was better than disappointing. The register was a never resolved uncertainty that gave the teacher much to ponder over in the slow, sleepless hours of the night. Widespread absence always came in waves and it seemed that as soon as one wave had spent itself, another arrived. The neat, herring-bone pattern of red marks in the register would yield gradually to round Os of sepulchral black, coming like the first heavy spots of a thunderstorm. Then, in a few more days the extent and nature of the new wave would be only too clear. Diphtheria; whooping cough; scarlet fever. In the winter months the incidence of serious illness came with daunting regularity and lasted for some weeks. Then, when spring came and sunnier days helped to remedy the ills of winter, of cold cottages and poor victuals, there was scarcely time for self-congratulation before the stone-picking season began. In April and May, when the growing corn was still short and the ground reasonably dry, came the traditional time for the tenderest of youngsters to bend their backs in the fields while the register solemnised their absence with rows of great black Os.

'Sixteen children,' wrote the headmistress of Hempston at a time when singing in school was still a novelty, 'are absent and engaged in stone-picking. Taught the children a hymn: Hold the Fort.'

3

HARVEST AND HARD TIMES

Stephen J. Crovier   —1995—

BY the time the school was whole again and scholars sitting properly in their places the year was gone and the register would be gaping its shortcomings once more to the visiting inspector. There was little chance, either, of the new school year beginning any better than the last. The summer holiday never seemed long enough for the harvest which would spread itself over the bad weather and into September before the stooks were taken in. Many a time it happened that the village school would reopen for the autumn term and discover that nothing could be done but to close it again. The

29

harvest had precedence over all things and teacher and School Board had to bow to the inevitable.

As for the scholars, the harvest brought them visible benefits – new boots, perhaps, or winter coats or dress material but such things were not important beside the vital experience of harvest itself. It was not something about which to be merely acquisitive but completely immersed, together with the family and the village. From their earliest days the children understood how significant the harvest was to life and livelihood and learned to see the harvest field as the true reality. It was the need and the struggle and the triumph of their simple lives. It was also a measure of growing up, with manliness coming with aching muscles, the gulping of drinks and scoffing of extra food in the warm sun, with small, eager fingers rasped by the straw and with the sense of excitement and power using the great horses and waggons.

A boy no higher than the nostrils of a giant Suffolk horse could manage to lead it, stumbling and leaning away from the splaying hoofs to bring the waggon along between the rows of stooks. It saved the men's time in tossing the sheaves. When the waggon came abreast of two more stooks the midget boy would shout and pull the rein hard beside the slavering mouth. Astonishingly, the great beast would stop and pant and spend the interval in turning its head to see what kind of miniature was there. Pitchforks would flail on both sides of the waggon again and the sheaves build up neatly all round the sides for the concave arrangement that would carry the load safely home. To move on, the boy would gather all the importance of his task into a high-pitched yell: 'Hold tight!' and would see the leader far above on the straw settle himself against the support of his pitchfork as the waggon jerked forward again.

At the end of the row of stooks there would be ropes thrown over the load and the boy would climb up the ropes to the very top to lie and cling to the shifting straw as the sky moved above his face. He would feel the waggon load beneath as it rolled and billowed and see nothing but the clouds, the turning and sliding of the silent clouds. Then suddenly the movement would stop and he would look down and see the familiar stackyard and the men looking up as they took off the ropes.

The voices come up to him as if from a long way off. 'He can take the loose hoss back to the field, can't he?' 'He ain't man enough, I doubt.' 'He's man enough – he can ride that hoss back while we unload and save a lot o' time.' 'Nar, he ain't man enough, I doubt.'

'Course I am,' he shouts, and slides down back into the reality where the great horse is taken out of the shafts and stands immense in its glittering, jangling accoutrements. 'Up you go,' the men shout. The boy half-turns with a question but the men slap the horse's rump and turn away. The back is acres broad and cluttered with harness and lines. The horse moves, bumping easily across the yard, ears askance at the doubtful signals from the rider. It carries him out of the yard, along the lane. There is nothing to it – it is like being a king or a knight setting off to battle. The horse moves and rattles the shining buckles and no one would dare to get in its way. The boy is a king high up above everyone else.

In the field the workers note the diminutive rider and go on with their tasks. At the spare waggon he slithers down and the horse is put into the shafts, the great feet moving delicately backward. Then, both horse and kingship are forgotten as toiling figures move suddenly in answer to a shout. Boys with knobbed sticks rush excitedly after the rabbit that has broken cover. If it is caught it will go to join the long row of bodies lying under the tree, for here at Hempston the custom is for the spoils to be divided up at the end of the day, according to accepted priorities which can scarcely be said to be equitable but which generally provided even the least of the boys with one rabbit to take home. On a good day it could be a pair, with legs professionally threaded one through another and dangling over the shoulder from the rabbiting stick. It was something that made the boy

Stephen. J. Govier. 1995.

forget his tired muscles – the very fact and proof of a triumphant day.

But there were reasons other than the agricultural seasons for gaps and dwindling numbers in the school register. During the eighties no fewer than 16 families left the village and were not replaced. Four of the families were removed to the workhouse. The long golden age had come to an end somewhere in the mid-seventies and the hard times had begun. For my grandparents, as for many others, life became a struggle to keep together and independent of the Poor Law Guardians. The growing desolation of the countryside was miserably reflected in the family in Church Cottage and one burden that became more and more difficult to bear was the payment of the school pence.

When it became impossible because it was likely to bring real hunger to the children, the situation had to be declared and the headmistress duly applied to the Union for assistance. The arrangement was that where a family was provenly so poor that it could not pay the school fees, then the workhouse would do so. I am sad to say that in the village records are the names of three children whose fees were so paid and these were Ellen and Henry, together with the next of the family, Frank.

It is impossible now to know all the details surrounding the bare record but the difficulties that my grandparents must have known and the ignominy they must have suffered at the hands of the probing Union man and of the neighbours is very real in my mind. How close they were, the whole family, to being taken to the workhouse I can only imagine. All I know for certain is that for a year or two the headmistress of the school made out a quarterly account for the three scholars – for all three of them a matter of only six shillings and sixpence – and sent it to the clerk at the Union for payment. The effect that such ignominy had on this proud family is recounted in the next chapter.

Perhaps it is bound to be a gloomy thing to search into a family's history. In seeking information about the school life of my aunts and uncles, I started up another wan ghost of a boy who must have been their cousin. His existence is barely recorded but scored with melancholy – once in the church register, put down among more respectable baptisms as 'base-born' – and once in the school records. Here, all that is said of him is that he 'cannot do much because of his eyes'. I wonder what happened to him, base-born and weakling when only the strong survived, and what miseries there were for him and his unfortunate mother in the cruel, religious arrogance of the village. The resigned note of the record shows that little in the way of physical care was expected of the school in 1879. In larger schools, it is said, there was a box of assorted spectacles from which a pair would be taken at random to deal with any complaint about poor eyesight. At Hempston there was nothing but the mere mention. I hope that someone at least sorrowed and cared for him.

Perhaps it is absurd to feel sorry for children who lived long ago, who grew up and spent their lives and have died. But the picture of them, like the still pictures of old silent films, is clear and real enough to me. As they walked again and again through the country lanes to school I have caught them in retrospect and held their hands and tried not to notice their rags and their degradation. They saw the same trees and the same fields that I see, but with different eyes and different experience. Good or bad, they took their leave before our own times and the plenty we would offer them is of no use. Their ghostly hands are grubby and empty – perhaps they suffered not a bit, knowing nothing of the future – perhaps the little they had was enough.

My father, who was a younger member of the family, often told us anecdotes of his early life and of the many episodes that proved himself to have been a 'sharper', though few relate to his school life. Nor is there any school record of his scholarship. From this heavy silence I have come to believe that both he and his teachers agreed that cleavage at the earliest possible moment would be happiest for everybody. His education, he claimed, came from attending night school after he left the village.

There was one incident that he remembered and told me late in life that happened at the time when there were six or seven children at home. Grandfather had come home from work one Saturday without wages. It was six o'clock in the evening and Grandmother and the brood were waiting to begin the meal of dumplings with rabbit stew. Throughout the meal Grandfather ate in silence, thinking of the long week he had worked and of the feckless character of his employer who had apparently gone off on a drinking spree and forgotten to pay him. Afterwards, as he sat in his chair by the fire wondering what he should do, Grandmother brought out the flour sack from the pantry and showed him that it was quite empty. She had used the last cupful or two for the dumplings, she told him, there was no bread in the house and not a mite of anything to make a meal. Grandfather again put on his coloured neckerchief and Grandmother brought his heavy boots and buskins.

Four or five of the children followed him as he left the cottage and walked down the lane to the farm. There, he harnessed one of the horses to a waggon while the children clambered up over the sides and sat on the floor. Grandfather saw them there and went back to the barn for an armful of sacks for them to sit on. Then he set off to find the farmer.

It was a late September evening and fine and dry. For several miles of the journey the children were in high spirits but as the dusk came down they began to huddle together in the sacks. Long before the waggon had reached the destination it was quite dark. Grandfather knew there was a public house that his farmer boss frequented and after some enquiries found out where it was. He pulled the waggon into the yard and got down. Although it was an inn where labourers were not welcome to mix with the farmers, Grandfather walked straight in and searched through the public rooms only to be told that the farmer had moved on to another public house outside the town.

After inquiring from passers-by, Grandfather managed to locate the inn and there he discovered his employer in the taproom with some of his cronies.

'Evening, master,' said Grandfather with respectful firmness. 'I'd like my wages if you please.' Half stupefied, the farmer stared at him.

'Hev you come all this way jest for that?' he asked at last. 'You could a-had it come Monday.'

'I got eight mouths to feed,' answered Grandfather. 'They don't stop eating on a Sunday.'

Some of the farmers were making comments about paying wages at the proper time and Grandfather's boss took him aside. 'That's a rum job tonight,' he said. 'I'm nearly spent out. The best thing I can think of is to go along to Jackson's mill over in Ashington. Ask him for a sack of flour and tell him it's for me. Do you try that.'

Grandfather had a rough idea where Jackson's mill was,

but there wasn't much light to go by except the stars and a candle lantern each side of the waggon. The journey seemed to continue for miles along strange roads and dark country lanes before he found the place. The children were quiet, as miserably tired of the endless jolting as of cold, but they roused themselves to peer over the side of the waggon as the miller came out. He was carrying a lantern and lifted it to look at Grandfather. When he heard the name of the farmer he became angry.

'He's got no right to send you over here for flour,' he grumbled. 'He owes me money already. I can't afford to supply him with stuff he don't pay for.'

Grandfather was too proud and too tired to argue. He walked stiffly back to the horse and began to turn the waggon around when the miller caught sight of half-a-dozen small white faces looking at him over the side.

'Hold on a minute, mister,' he called to Grandfather. He came closer and shone the light into the children's faces. They were pinched and still with cold and fright. He stepped back and told Grandfather: 'You back your cart up to the barn door. I'll give you a sack o' flour an' welcome, no matter what sort o' boss you've got. But do you get them poor little owd kids home in the warm.'

With the sack of flour and a piece of canvas tilt that the miller had stretched over the children, Grandfather set off on the long journey home. By the time he got back to the farm it was nearly midnight. He bedded the horse down and carried the flour on his shoulder to the cottage.

Grandmother had got the oven hot and the tins were warming in front of the range. Without a word, she got to work on making the dough and none of the children, save the youngest, was rash enough to ask for food before they went to bed. For the youngest Grandfather took a penny out of his pocket and asked him if he wouldn't rather have the penny than his supper. In the morning Grandmother would get the penny back by offering him the 'biggest' breakfast in exchange.

Stephen J Sovek 1995

Grandfather stayed up in the kitchen until the smell of the fine new loaves began to fill the house. Come daylight, he would make the rounds of his illicit snares along the edge of the glebe land and with luck the family would have full stomachs before the church bell called them all to the Sunday service.

For on Sunday all questions and hardships had to be resolved or forgotten. No matter how desperate and earthy had been the commerce before – on Sunday an air of sanctity descended and the poverty that had been merely economic all through the week now became a way of salvation. Genteel piety became the centre of existence. Even objects of unimportance, which had been passive all the week – like the chenille tablecloth with tassels that was kept out of sight in a drawer, the scented soap that must not normally be used for merely dirty hands, the pressed gloves and the prayer books that waited on the little table by the parlour window, the blackinged boots in the porch – all these suddenly became Sunday.

Activities, too, without much significance when they were made, the starching and gophering, polishing and ironing, sewing and darning that kept the women of the family busy long evenings through now showed their purpose in the pattern of Sunday respectability. Other things there were – the clean smell of lavender bags disturbed in the deep chests of drawers; dresses that rustled; the scrubbed worn bricks of the porch still damp from diligent preparations; the men's buttonholes of garden flowers and, above all, the immense, dragging inactivity, all sacred to the Sabbath Day.

Such things, together with the gentle atmosphere of the day had a cathartic and rejuvenating effect on village folk. Labour and the spiritless struggle of daily life were disposed of somehow for a few hours and in their place came aspirations not only for a place in the parson's Heaven but even more for nice, genteel, respectable things on earth. Even my Grandfather would join in this common metamorphosis, putting on some dark clothes and covering his leathern hands with gloves. But it was the women who sought most in this weekly transformation, using their gifts of achieving daintiness and grace with the least of material aids in order to taste the strange and envied world of genteel living.

With the Sabbath over, and gentility and God served for yet another week, Monday returned the family with ungentle haste to the realities of existence. For my Grandfather it meant being out of the cottage and into the fields by six o'clock; for the children there was a different kind of discipline and new masters to serve.

4

GAMES AND CHORES

Stephen J. Govier - 1995

PERHAPS because I can remember so well the cottage where my grandparents lived, the lane, the church and the village, it is not difficult in my mind to hear the click of the latch on the gate and to watch the growing brood of children as they set off for school. The way they took is still unchanged and quiet. The long grass fringes the lane and the willows down beside the river still whisper across the water meadows. Their exit from the gate and into the lane was into a morning with no sound. In the fields and on the turnpike itself there was a quiet that made significant and lonely their own voices, the rustlings of small creatures in the hedges and the drumming of the distant lock over the marshes.

The sand of the lane was loose and fine, as by some

miracle it still is, and long before the boys arrived at school their newly-blacked boots would be grey with dust, the girls' ribbons all awry with romping on the banks. Ellen would scold, forever dragging the most unwilling by the hand and settling their frocks and pinafores before they reached the gates. Sometimes, on summer mornings, they would forsake the sandy lane and take instead the grass-grown path called the Church Walk. It was stoutly held by those who preferred this way that it was a short cut, though no one else seemed to think so. The real attraction was in the abundance of natural excitements that it provided – birds and their nests, dragonflies and butterflies – things to see and hear in the undisturbed hedges.

It was exciting in other ways, too, for they must turn off from the Church Walk and enter the churchyard with its melancholy rows of headstones, skirting the church porch with careful steps on the gravel. Then – the final part of the journey – a wild scoot across the paddock in front of the Rectory in a delicious fear that the Rector or his wife might be watching from the windows. At this stage the girls' dolls would be carried frenziedly by their ankles and boys in hard, tight collars looked likely to burst in the mad haste. They were, in fact, never seen from the Rectory; or if seen, never reprimanded. Perhaps there was never any need for their hurry except in their imagination.

I believe they all did well at school. The girls won prizes and Ellen became a model pupil and a teacher's pet. In the logbook of the school it is recorded that on 13th October 1876 she was made a monitor at only nine years of age and that, for this responsibility she was excused the payment of school fees, or 'pence'. A little later, when the cleaner became ill, she went to the school early and late, sweeping and dusting the school rooms for payment of sixpence a week.

The new red bricks of the school were as yet unmarked. It would take decades of scholars to gouge and pry with blunted penknives, to kick and prod with their waiting heels, before such brick declined to a more amenable condition in which initials could be carved and pencils sharpened and friendly relationships begun. At that time, the bricks proclaimed the sequestered nature of scholarship as they supported the tall lean windows and the reed-thatched roof and turned themselves about so as to be visible also in the interior, thinly camouflaged in dark green distemper.

Even more forbidding were the walls of the outer perimeter of the playgrounds, with heavy iron gates that breached them at each end. Ellen would take the boys to the gate at the far end and abandon them, not without misgivings, to the male confusion within. In this ante-room of the school the learning was crude but easily remembered through the regular accompaniment of bruises and torn clothes which Ellen would try to deal with before they reached home.

On either side of the separating wall between boys and girls, the noise and activity continued until a monitor came to pull the long rope of the bell hanging above the main porch. At the first sound the scholars arranged themselves stiffly in rows beside the appropriate door while the schoolmistress appeared in the gloomy entrance at the boys' side, a figure in black, remote and unamused. Monitors straightened the lines of waiting scholars, turned them inexorably towards enlightenment and marched them in. Once inside, the children settled themselves in their appointed places in the dry, unaffectionate atmosphere of compelled learning.

There were three classrooms, separated from the main hall by wooden partitions which could be folded – with some difficulty – with glass panes at a height which allowed the headmistress to peer in from time to time to see that all was as it should be. In their separate boxes the captured ones watched the sun climb and swing in its great arc across the windows. By the time of their release in the late afternoon it would have dropped low into the western sky and to untamed children of nature it must have seemed that a whole lifetime had passed them by as they sat at their despised desks.

Halfway through the morning, a short break brought the scholars tumbling out into the open air, making sure to put on their hats and bonnets against the dangers of sunstroke or – according to the weather – double pneumonia. The playground had no permanent surface and had never been properly levelled but was beaten to a certain degree of uniformity by the battering of restless feet in hobnailed boots. On this rough surface they no doubt engaged in the same immense, inconsequential activities that occupy children in any playground where they find themselves thrown together with time to waste. If it were possible to find a pattern or some dominating motive for the frantic activity of a playground it would probably be that of a chase, of hunter and hunted, capture and escape, victory and defeat – with endless spontaneous variations. Such games derive directly from the nature of children and especially of boys who, having lost the hopeless war with authority, must join battle with a lesser foe to regain their self-esteem. The playground, confined as it was in time and space, provided an experience of immediate, volatile relationships. But for it, many children who would have known very little about play were now caught up in these strange activities and shown what excitement was and laughter.

If traditional games were played, then ring marbles would be one, while the girls hopped and skipped and sang the verses of long-known chanting games. Boys then, as now, were happy to scuff around with a ball or indeed with any object considered mobile. If nothing better was available, a bundle of closely-tied rags or paper could be used for a short spell and they seldom missed the opportunity of inflating a pig's bladder for a football. Such meagre equipment might now be regarded as deprivation – to the cottage parents it was nonsense enough and to spare. Encouraging children to waste time playing seemed to be yet another way in which the school was alienating them. Certainly there would be no question of what sort of activity would occupy the scholar when he arrived home in the afternoon. The daily chores of

Stephen J. Govier · 1995

a rural family were numerous and heavy and all the members beyond infancy had their allotted tasks. If children were ill-advised enough to think they could continue with a game after arriving home, they would soon be brought back to earth, perhaps with a ringing clout on the ear. Necessity and high spirits did not go well together. Mother gave the initial orders and the summary punishment; final authority lay with the father, who in those days, believed that a boy's wayward spirit had to be curbed and a bit of sense knocked into him as much for his own future good as for the peace and good-standing of the family.

Prominent in the backyard of each cottage was the great chopping-block derived from some massive tree bole and which had become scored and moulded to a diminishing roundness as small boys cut more and yet more kindling for the fires. Of all tasks in the minor ages this was the most important, most regular and most difficult to escape, for the whole domestic organisation depended on it. Early in the morning, every morning, the kitchen range must be lit for the needs of the day and woe betide a boy whose sticks were wet or green or too thick to ignite. Worse still for the boy who had neglected the task altogether.

After wood – water. At Grandfather's cottage, clear spring water was drawn up from a well with a bucket and rope on a windlass. This, too, was a job for older boys but the lesser members would often watch to see the bucket of shivering-cold water appear like magic out of the deep hole. On hot days they would run to get the enamel mug to dip in and taste the icy wonder of it. But such water, though so good, was not suitable for the family's washing and rain-water had to be brought in from the pond or from the butts that stood at the corner of the house.

It was a boy's place in the yard and a girl's to help in the house or to run errands. Whatever the errand, it was usually a welcome respite from other chores. The boy who was chopping sticks or cleaning boots or fetching water might well look enviously as his sister set off for the skimmed milk from the farm, especially as such expeditions were usually helped along by a thick piece of bread and jam. It was a chance, too, for a girl to take a skipping rope or a hoop if she wanted to get along the lane quickly or, on lazy spring and summer days, to pick flowers from the banks for a posy. Going to the shop was nice enough but better still to walk down the deep lane to the farm where the warm smells came to meet you and you walked through the nettice to the dairy and noticed how the milk lost its animal flavour in the clean coolness and became watery-smelling and delicate. In there the churns would be turning and the separator busily dispensing at the same time the cream for the Rectory and the skim milk for the cottagers.

There were other tasks to be done before Grandfather came home from work. Boys would disappear for a time to feed rabbits or ferrets or to collect eggs, little ones to clean the tallow from the candlesticks. It was Ellen who did the more important tasks, like filling the standing lamp with paraffin-oil and cleaning the fragile lamp-glass with a wisp of paper. The lamp would stand in the centre of the living-room table and wait for the dusk before it came to life.

In dark winter evenings they sat there in the yellow light by the table or dreamed in the firelight where it flickered in dark, cosy inglenooks. Grandmother would sit close beneath the lamp for her darning and sewing while Grandfather dozed in the tall wheel-back chair for a time. Then as like as not he would view the boys' boots with a very stern disapproving air and bring forth the last and shoe-makers' leather and set up a busy tapping before the fire, bending forward over the last, holding the tacks in his mouth until he needed them.

In all the other rooms the darkness waited. It waited to fight and chivvy the encroaching candlelight, following it closely, darting in if the flame faltered or fell. Candlesticks and a case full of spills stood on the mantelpiece in the living-room and those who took a candle, perhaps to put a hot baked brick into a frozen bed, or who lit the hurricane-lamp to light the way to the privy at the bottom of the garden, had the blackness at their heels to drive them back quickly to the hazy warmth and welcome of the living-room. When the young scholar went to bed, the darkness crowded the tiny circle of candlelight and hid the fancied demons in the corners of the room and under the bed when the candle was extinguished. Only a pampered few would have a nightlight to stay the horror; the rest could say their prayers again under the blankets and withstand the terrors of the darkness as best they could.

On every day of the week an urgent routine possessed the house and left its mark on the departing scholars. On Monday it was always washday, by inexorable decree. The brick copper that had been boiled up for the Saturday bath-night was filled again with soft rainwater and stoked up for the vast needs of a day in which even Grandfather had to make do for his midday meal. It was a day when any childish troubles were brushed aside by their elders and when only the washing finally triumphed. Grandmother wore her 'coarse' apron — a clean hessian sack — and baled the hot water from the copper to the tub to be churned with a dolly-peg and then scrubbed, garment by garment, with a hefty scrubbing-brush against the corrugated face of the board. The rinsing and soaping, the stoking and reboiling of the copper, the despatch of buckets of water to the garden and the elbow-deep fight to regain cleanliness, ensured day-long clouds of steam and smoke above the growing pools of water on the kitchen floor. The smell of wet clothes pursued the children to school and welcomed them back in the afternoon, with the mangle waiting to be turned by two boys together.

Not much less demanding was Tuesday, when the clothes must be dried — or Wednesday, when they must be ironed. Then there were the frantic cleaning days when rugs and mats of varied kinds were taken out into the garden to be solidly beaten with the copper-stick before the floors were scrubbed; when the kitchen range was cleared and black-leaded and the hearthstone whitened afresh; when doorsteps and windows, brass knobs and china figures and everything else in reach had to be polished and rejuvenated by various processes of which the common factor was the abundant use of 'elbow grease'. In mid-week, the house shook and clattered in preparation for settling down to a state of almost prudish correctitude, with a new asperity governing the entrance of muddy boots and the occupations of grubby fingers.

It was a condition short-lived, however, for on Fridays the smell of Ronuk and Brasso retreated before the new and warmer smells of baking. Fresh loaves spilled their golden crusts over the edges of the baking-tins and begged to be sampled before they were ranged side by side on the pantry shelves. On Fridays when the children came home a warm crust would sometimes reward their excited interest and if there was lard still from the last pig-killing they could have that too, spread over the crust with a topping of salt and mustard. Such was the opulence of Friday and the power of new bread that scholars retired replete and happy and had little complaint to make of indigestion the next morning. On Saturday all was changed. In the face of the coming Sabbath there was a fanatical need to have everything 'nice and straight', clean and respectable. The baking smells were scarcely allowed house-room in such sanctity, the signs of labour all put out of sight.

At the back of the cottage where my grandparents lived, there was a tiny porch no bigger than a sentry box, which was the no-man's land between the earthy world without and the cleanliness of the interior. In it were the brushes and brooms, the boot-scraper and the rough wooden bench holding tin bowl and soap. After a day's work on the farm, Grandfather would enter the kitchen from a short encounter with these objects looking tired but clean and presentable. Bootless, in striped flannel shirt and corduroy trousers still tied below the knees with leather bootlaces, he expected to sit down at once to the table and have his meal. Children had to wait until he arrived, making sure not to be sitting in his chair, nor indeed in any chair for very long.

In fact, even if there had been time for children to be lounging, there was little furniture to lounge on. In this, as in other things, a kind of puritanical expediency covered the limitations of poverty and labouring lives by recalling that slothfulness was one of the deadly sins. Lethargy was not merely an uneconomic condition in labouring life – it was irreligious. Only the head of the family would have the right, divine and domestic, to relax in the austere comfort of an armchair, which in those days meant a tall-backed wooden chair with a cushion on the seat. The only concession to supine comfort downstairs was the sofa – a craftily-shaped piece of furniture that allowed considerable comfort (and was invaluable for sickness and convalescence) without appearing to concede anything to moral weakness.

Luxury in the bedroom was a feather bed over a flock mattress, though the children might only have the latter. The bedsteads were of iron, brass-knobbed and durable, for after all this was the age of iron and concepts of permanence. Thin metal slats supported the mattress and provided a slight, scraping resilience which to tired people could have seemed a welcome springiness. The parental bed, with its frill or valance all round, shared a kind of persiflage with other objects in the home – the covering or camouflaging of whatever seemed indelicate or ungenteel. Nowadays we are too impatient of coyness to do more than scoff or laugh at such ideas. Nevertheless, it was important to people then. There was something in the times which caused even the poorest families to cover and decorate and entrench, to gather themselves within a cocoon bursting with treasured bric-à-brac. In some rooms already full of personal conceits a folding screen would be used to add privacy to privacy; windows that could have looked only on innocent country fields were not only lace-curtained but either shuttered or covered with opaque blinds. The cottage was enclosed and the domestic front embattled – but for what cause or against what enemy?

Whatever the motives of rural Victorians in their close-kept lives, it was this environment that the young scholars inherited. These were the standards that they took to school with them and which influenced their conduct and attitudes to others; when they grew up, their cottage upbringing brought them voluntarily to fight for the continuance of their way of life. Not until the twenties came and new generations of children sat in the schools was there a complete rejection of the old ways. By that time increasing freedom made it easy to forget how rigidly life in the villages had been controlled and how completely a family then had depended on local opinion. The parish boundaries were the boundaries of most people's experiences and within these limits it was expedient to keep to the customs and standards expected. Perhaps because a village was always looking in upon itself, these standards became ever more narrow and arbitrary as time went on and it is difficult to assess how much of the incessant struggle to appear respectable and without blemish came from the fear of intolerant gossip or church-backed disapproval.

The village gossips would tolerate poverty if it were respectable and well-darned since it was a condition common to many, but the workhouse, the last resort of the poor, was a different consideration altogether. It was the feckless and not merely unfortunate who were taken in, many thought. When gossip spread the news that the local workhouse was having to pay the school fees of three of Grandfather's children, the code of village standards was broken. From then on, the unhappy children carried a stigma – the smell of the workhouse was upon them. It was their shame at this, rather than their ragged clothing, that caused them to take more frequently the short cut to school by way of the churchyard and rectory paddock. They came to realise that the short cut had another advantage – you could reach the turnpike and the world beyond as well as the school without being seen by the village people from their cottage windows.

The time came when the two oldest boys, Henry and Frank, then 13 and 12 years old, felt that they had endured long enough the jeers of their school-mates and the unmitigated poverty at home. At daybreak one morning, with no more than a few scraps of food in their pockets, they took the short cut for the last time. They were seen on the turnpike heading away from Hempston and were given a lift on a milk-cart. Then they vanished. Whatever experiences they encountered in the next few days can only be imagined, for there is no record to go by and my grandparents never mentioned their names except in a quiet, private way to each other that discouraged any questions. All that is known is that they were picked up three weeks later as waifs and strays and within a month were sent by some charitable organisation to do farm work in Australia.

The first news that Grandfather ever had was a letter received two years after the boys left home. It was signed by both boys and carried the address of a Queensland sheep station. 'Just a few lines,' it said in the traditional formula of rural correspondence, 'to say we hope you are all well as it leaves us the same.'

It was the Black Year when the boys left the village, the year when the slump in farming was accentuated by bad weather to such an extent that it seemed that nature had turned on those who ministered to it. Not only had prices fallen, with foreign corn and meat taking away the island security that had so long supported these products but the harvest, that might have brought some recompense had it been a good one, failed completely. Corn rotted in the fields in the interminable rain. Sheep, for so long kept as part of the good husbandry of arable land, fell in thousands to the bane of foot-rot and had to be destroyed. Not only one bad harvest, either, but three in succession with extreme periods of rain and alternate drought that brought the long decline from the golden age of farming down to the ultimate rock-bottom.

Step by step the farmer was dragged downwards; from a prosperous livelihood to a struggling but still hopeful existence, then to an enforced living off capital and finally to a desperate effort to get out without losing everything. As for tenant farmers with less capital at risk, the time soon came when the less efficient and less well-placed could do no more than leave house, buildings and land to become derelict. I remember being told that one could walk for miles in the early nineties without finding a single tenanted farm – all were empty and deserted.

Only the bargain hunters now bought farms. To Pightle, for example, which was one of the model farms in the area in its best days, came the ignominy of being sold to a dealer in rabbit skins for £15 an acre, which was a third of what the owner had paid 20 years before. When Cowgate Farm came up for sale in 1893 villagers could remember how this once prosperous farm had cost the owner the considerable sum of £13,000. Now, it hung fire for months until desolate necessity dared not laugh at the offer of £1,850 and the farm changed hands for this amount.

With the prosperity of the farms went also the stability of village life. Perhaps the two boys were wiser than they knew in leading what became a massive exodus of country folk from the village in order to seek better conditions elsewhere. For those who chose to remain, wages were reduced and the situation became grim indeed.

5

HYMNS AND TREATS

Stephen J. Gower. 1995.

WHEN the Black Year came and the years after, the family in Church Cottage came to know just how desperate the times were. Food was expensive and wages low; wet days were unpaid and nothing but a man's wits and energy lay between what the farmer chose to pay and the fact of hunger. Many a story has been told to me of ways they used to keep the wolf from the door; of outwitting game-keepers and farmers in the deadly game of poaching in which an instant's carelessness could cost a man both job and home; of sitting down with a hungry family on bad days with no more to feast on than a boiling of swedes stolen from the field; of trying to ease the hunger of young bellies with bread dipped in hot salt water; of going down to the slaughterhouse for half a sheep's head or the chance of cheap offal.

No wonder that the scholars of the eighties and nineties, driven to school by the School Board man, came obstinate and hungry as wild things and found little to satisfy them in the kind of food it gave. They were lean and sharp and their wits were needed in other matters than book-learning. In fact, nothing in their own environment prepared them to submit to school-work or to impersonal learning of any kind. Their impatience with the lot of scholar led them bitterly and desperately into raw conflict with their teachers, whose unbending authority was supported by immediate and rigorous chastisement.

As it happened, the dreariness of school life was by now beginning to ease a little, though still within the confines of the payment-by-results system. Scripture and the three Rs still had precedence and the same pattern of dull, repetitive learning had to be endured, but a little sweetness and light had been introduced into the long grim days by the teaching of singing. So welcome was this innovation to teacher and pupil alike that the learning of a song or a new hymn tune was regarded as being of sufficient moment to be recorded in the school logbook. Sometimes it appeared in unexpected juxtaposition with other information. For example: 'Taught the children a new hymn – Now the Day is Over. The eldest boy in the school kept in until 8 pm for disobedience.'

The entry could be one to smile over but for a shock at the period of detention. Was it really eight o'clock in the evening before the boy was released? What was so heinous in his lack of obedience that he should be robbed, this wayward scholar, of a whole summer's evening? And what would he do in all that time – read the Bible? Learn the Catechism? Take out the worn reader and repeat it over again? What of all the activities that awaited him at home – the checking of snares, searching for hens' eggs, cleaning out the rabbits?

Stephen. J. Govier - 1995-

A glance at the date on which this luckless boy was kept in shows his penance to be even worse than suspected, for this was on 7th August. The harvest would be in full swing and perhaps audible to him in the quiet school. All the excitements that might have made the day endurable were for others. It must have seemed a long, long time for the day to be over for this boy – a day that perhaps he remembered, as well as the hymn tune, for the rest of his life.

Another innocent association of hymn title and comment was made by the new mistress of a school not far from Hempston. On her very first day she wrote: 'Taught a hymn – There is a Happy Land, Far, Far Away. Many are absent working in the fields.'

Perhaps these were what people might nowadays call Freudian slips: certainly the records contained in school logbooks are as illuminating about hymn relationships as about academic facts. Every teacher saw school life in a different way and accordingly accented the priority. From one there are comments on attendance recurring so regularly that they give an impression of acute anxiety; from others the keynote may be conduct or school fees or the lack of books. Punishment is recorded, though perhaps not always, and the cane given most frequently for bad language and blasphemy.

Sometimes it was the difficulties caused by structural defects or even by vagaries of nature that upset the routine of an early school and so became the subjects of logbook entries. At Thorpham, for instance, the school was closed from time to time for as long as three days because the wind was in the 'wrong' direction and was blowing the smoke down the chimney. Perhaps the pupils on their way to this school hopefully held up their wetted fingers to discover if the wind was coming from the right (or 'wrong') quarter and likely to provide them with a holiday. At Asthorpe there was another regular hazard: 'The school door handle is off, in consequence of which we are occasionally imprisoned and have to push a boy through a window in order that he may find someone to come to the rescue.'

It was the logbook that duly reflected the enormous interest and relief at the advent, in later years, of a new and totally different subject for the erstwhile scholar – the simple but revolutionary idea of the Object Lesson, little enough to become madly gay over, perhaps, but something that showed a glimmer of light at the end of the tunnel. Pupil teachers and veterans alike welcomed the innovation as sheer relief from the oppressive grind, and lightened spirits invest the logbooks of the time with something like excitement. Now, it is no longer the new hymn tune that merits a mention but the chosen object of the week. Enthusiastic teachers would not only proclaim the object for the current week but objects to come for the whole term and beyond. The scope was un-limited: A Cat; A Candle; A Pair of Shoes; A Leaf; A Bar of Soap, and so on, with the very advanced idea of making an all-round study and only indirect reference to the tools of reading and writing. For the first time, perhaps, teacher and scholar were able to reach common ground without repression and without hostility.

The first of the practical subjects to be added to the timetable was sewing and its attendant skills. Darning was considered a most useful accomplishment and prizes were often given for this and for knitting. 'Two of the girls,' a logbook claims with a note of triumph, 'have commenced to knit stockings.' Perhaps for a few years the boys had to follow the treadmill of the three Rs while the girls enjoyed the wild pleasure of darning socks and making pinafores.

As if to compensate for such levities, the Annual Code (from the central Education Department) decided that in future the whole of the Church Catechism must be learned in its entirety. It showed that in the old National and British schools the hand of the Church was as strong as ever and in the new elementary schools a considerable influence. Support from Victorian public opinion continued to sustain, not only for piety's sake but in the belief that religion served to discipline the poor and to curb any excessive ambitions that they might have. The regular thanking of God for that state of life in which He thought fit to place them was considered proper and fitting. So there was the catechism, the collects, the creeds, the psalms and the Bible – and no end to the memorising, encouraged as it was by the local clergy and visiting bigwigs who would handsomely bestow a prize on a child who showed proper respect for God and the gentry.

At Hempston the clergyman was a regular visitor, listening to the chanted questions and answers of the catechism, examining on the Bible and possibly teaching a new prayer, though all with growing perfunctoriness until the real purpose of his visits seemed to be the lengthy consideration of the register and the occasional beating of small boys whom the headmistress felt it unseemly to cane.

Other visitors were plentiful, though less from strictly educational motives than in the tradition of country gentlefolk. Scarcely a day passed but that the clergyman's wife popped in with some wool and stayed to hear the little ones sing a hymn; or the squire's sister looked in, perhaps from sheer ennui, and examined the needlework or the copybooks; or the wealthy spinster ladies from the Old Manor came in to bring some sweets and to stay for an hour or so.

However cynically we may look on such benevolence now, they were given – and accepted – in good faith at that time when so little care and kindness came the way of the poor family. There is no doubt that many of the local difficulties of the early schools generally were smoothed by the attentions of the old order of gentlefolk and there was one day each year when villagers one and all were ready to say 'Thankye kindly' to the nobs. This was the day of the School Treat.

From long custom, the Treat at Hempston was held in the grounds of the Old Manor – until that place became overgrown from neglect and the two spinster ladies too old to welcome the noise. The Rectory garden was too small and the grounds of the Hall resolutely unobtainable; in the end the venue was fixed in the surrounds of an ancient abbey a few miles away. There was an extra charm about this site, for not only was there the excitement of travelling in farm waggons but the abbey itself was believed to be haunted.

On the day, ever warm and mellow in the memories of those who took part, the scholars would assemble on the common close to the school, watch for the waggons and horses, unbelievably gay in ribbons and brasses, and scramble to sit in the best places. A score of children could sit on the straw that cushioned the worn floors and a dozen or more on the broad sides that were built to carry great loads of sheaves. A happy few were able to dangle their legs over the tailboard and watch the road draw away from beneath them. All would be dressed in their best, washed and ironed and combed and sashed for all to see.

The delights of such a day were simple and rarely recorded save when old men come to recall the pleasures of summers long ago. Nevertheless the happiness was real and rare, with unaccustomed excitements and privileges, races across the soft, green turf and sweets for prizes, the wonder of pretty dresses and of seeing elegant ladies being friendly to mothers and, after all, the Scramble. The benefactors came with great bags of sweets and flung them like scattered corn all over the grass and everyone smiled to see the scrambling mêlée of bodies intent on reaping the harvest no matter the cost.

Then there was the journey home with the great wheels turning and crunching the flint on the quiet road, and the girls sitting high up brushing the overladen hedgerows with their straw hats and the boys counting their treasure in the bottom of the waggon. When they got to the Green they would all shout and sing their excitement into waiting village ears. Not on that day, perhaps, did they yearn for other things – this world was good enough.

The little school at Hempston is empty now and it tells nothing of the agonies of generations of scholars who sat and held their heads at the old desks and plodded their way into literacy, then gone their ways. The children from the Church Cottage attended the school over a period of something like 15 years before the last name was omitted from the register.

Ellen, the star pupil, put up her hair and went into service, at first nearby then at houses further and further from the village until it became a place too far and too well-remembered to visit. The two boys who had gone to Australia were almost followed by Alfred, the third son, who got as far as Liverpool and found a job there and stayed. Sarah, the loved second daughter, came home in shame when she was only 17 and dared not stay to face the village gossips, took the short cut at night and stumbled over the gravestones in the churchyard, running even then across the Rectory paddock. Where she went and how she fared, no one knows and of the rest of the family of 12 only the parish record of births, marriages and deaths gives the bare bones of their lives.

6

INTO THE TWENTIES

SOMETIME around the year 1924, when I was 12 years old, I reached the considerable plateau of Standard Four in the National School at Woodbridge. For some reason it was always called the Blue School as opposed to the Yeller School – a British School about a mile away. Both, of course, were now included in the general status of Elementary Schools.

That year is fixed for me by a photograph that I still have. It shows a group of about 35 vastly assorted characters whose only common feature is the grimly wondering expression on their faces. With the big and more untidy boys at the back and small girls sitting in front, the assemblage presents an array of styles and tastes in clothing that has moved only a few degrees from those of their mothers and fathers in the nineties. There are still boys with ragged elbows and torn trouser seats and girls with pinafores and high button boots but also some who show the new ideas that befit the moving times of the twenties.

On a fine clear day in 1924 this little group was brought together in the playground and waited there while the photographer prepared himself with tripod and plates and hid under the black cover before they froze for the vital moment. No matter what fates have scattered them since, the old photograph still holds them solidly together in the playground and it needs little effort of memory on my part to join them there.

Best remembered are those who came 'our way' to school; one of these was Sally. She lived in a weather-boarded hut so small that it was a mystery how her parents were always hidden away within. Despite their invisibility, however, Sally

appeared each morning clean and shining, always with a great bow of ribbon in her hair, thin-legged and for ever out of reach. She ran straight home to the little bungalow after school and hardly ever came out to play. In the photograph she stands at the very edge of the group as if even then she was preparing to set her thin legs in motion again and race out of sight.

And there, in the back row, is Shorty Adams – the tall thin boy in a collarless flannel shirt held at the neck by a brass collar-stud. Shirt collars were always a problem, solved by some mothers by using the hard celluloid kind that could be easily washed or by buying the new woollen guernseys. For Shorty and his kind, unfortunately, there could be no such fal-de-lals. On the few occasions that he had ever been constrained into wearing a collar it obviously provided some special kind of torture for him. He wore an old loose jacket that could have been a coat, some cut-down corduroy trousers and, in common with two or three of his cronies, he sported a basic type of haircut that consisted of having his head shorn almost to the scalp except for a brush or fringe in front. With such haircuts, when the nurse came on her regular visits to examine heads for nits, the quarry was at least restricted to this area and not living in riotous abandon as in the hair of two or three of the girls.

Among them was untidy little Florrie Bent, with her frizzy hair and frizzy features, Sarah Swan who was cold and thin as if with perpetual fright, and stubby little Muriel Perriman who had a wild-dog reputation because 'she bit'. All of these were notorious carriers of nits and were sometimes sent home to wash their hair. Not so Connie and Betty, sitting together like lovebirds in the very centre of the group, their ribbons slipping on to each other's shoulders. These two enjoyed one of those inviolate friendships that lasted throughout their schooldays – Betty, clean and nervous and old-fashioned, Connie in her high boots and pinafore.

Joe, Hoss, Winkle and Kitch sit together, as one would expect. For once they are quiet, for once hatless. Joe's trousers, so perennially torn that he exhibits his shirt-tails almost as a way of life, are fortunately out of sight but his rolled-up cloth cap looks from his pocket. Kitch sits with undiminished glory in the centre of the gang, though it must have been about this time that he faced a considerable threat to his status with the arrival of a new boy named Verdun.

Among others who went along with us to school were four boys from a village some four miles away. For some reason their parents had become disenchanted with their local school and the boys were made to walk the journey from their home to the Blue School. It was unusual to have children from outside the neighbourhood and these exiles, paying the price of being foreigners, were forced into many an unfair fight with the natives. It was a bit of swank, it seemed to us, that they should carry satchels, just like grammar school boys, and even when we discovered that the satchels only carried their sandwiches and tea bottle, the resentment remained, only partly discounted by the fact that the boys were very good at football.

At that time there was no provision either for milk or for meals at school and the four boys sat in the classroom and ate their sandwiches by the fire in the winter with the special permission of the headmaster. In the warmer months they were turned out and you could sometimes see them dashing about the school gardens with massive bread 'doorsteps' crumbling from their hands and choking them as they ran.

There was then a sanctified two-hour break in the middle of the school day when everyone, teacher and pupil alike, (except for the exiles) left the building deserted and a period of detached serenity fell upon playground and classroom. At 12 noon the children would be dismissed after the singing of grace to the tune of the 'Old Hundred' and they would disappear almost by magic, as children always do when presented with the opportunity of freedom. Teachers were able to make their way sedately home – walking-sticks were considered to be a prop to dignity – and to enjoy a well-ordered lunch routine and a rest before setting forth again for the afternoon session. It is doubtful if they ever imagined that the time would come when teachers and children would be locked together in a midday crescendo of noise and activity, or if they did, must have put the thought aside as a touch of after-dinner dyspepsia.

At two o'clock the amnesty was over. Children reappeared with less speed than they had dispersed and teachers climbed on to their high stools to mark the registers. At the end of the afternoon the four exiles were always first out of school and well up the road, with satchels bouncing on their rumps as they hurried to get over the first mile or so of the journey home. It was not often that they got a lift, except in a farm tumbril and this was a very doubtful boon since it was slow and bumpy and usually smelling of new farmyard manure. Sometimes they were lucky enough to get a lift in a market cart; at other times they might beg a ride on a friend's bicycle, one foot balanced on the spindle that projected from the back hub and a knee resting uncomfortably on the carrier. Except on a convenient decline, however, such transport was of little value, making life exceedingly difficult for both the passenger and the unfortunate who was pedalling in front.

We who were on the country side of the school were all rudely healthy and well-fed. It was from the other direction, the rows of cramped houses in the back streets of the town, that children came pinched-looking and old. They would have seemed out of place had they taken our rural way home. Nevertheless, they were the real characters of the school and our friends in unshakeable loyalty.

I know now what happened eventually to nearly all of Standard Four. In a separate compartment of my mind I know that they moved out of that frozen group in the photograph and became other people. Shorty must have taken to a collar eventually and Joe to trousers that concealed his shirt tails for they both took the army uniform, were captured together at Singapore and did not return. Sergeant Hoss and Private Winkle also lost their lives with honour in the eastern sphere of a war that Standard Four had not even dreamed about. Frightened Sarah Swan was 'put away' and several others have died. An elderly, respectable-looking woman spoke to me one day a few years ago and claimed that she was Betty. It was a piece of information that meant nothing to me. So far as I am concerned, Betty was and is the little girl in the picture — as are all the others. Whatever happened to them after, it was to the twenties that they belonged, where they felt the sun that spring day and shouted their gladness along the quiet roads. How it was they came to die or to grow old is something that belongs to a different world altogether.

Sally, the elusive Sally, was the only girl in the group with short hair. The rest wore their hair loose and long, satisfied when it reached their waists, pleased to adorn it with slides and ribbons and unaware that scissors were already being made and sharpened that would send them bobbed and shingled into the emancipated future. A revolution was coming, though we scarcely recognised it in Standard Four of the National School. The bobbing of hair was not the heart of it any more than the knitting of the old women by the French guillotine represented that more bloody struggle. But the sign was there to read and to build on. By the end of the twenties an immense change – personal and domestic rather than cataclysmic – had altered the attitudes of a century. Short hair was nothing, except that in the same gesture so much else of the past was thrown aside.

Perhaps it all began as early as 1906 with that small but welcome shower of beneficences provided by the Liberal Government when for the first time some of the fear of going hungry or of being forced into the workhouse was removed. Modest health insurance, old-age pensions (five shillings for those over 70) and school care for the physical well-being of children represented something fundamentally new in the attitude of authority to the poor. Now the whole family, not least the scholars themselves, could draw both material and psychological benefits from the new ideas of social responsibility which included a growing, though still grudging, respect for common education. It was a different, an optimistic but not entirely emancipated kind of pupil who sat in the classrooms of the nineteen-twenties.

In Standard Four of the National School we were scarcely a pampered breed but we had a history of school-going behind us now and we benefited, too, from the reactions to the First World War. We had taken part in the incredible domestic upheaval of mothers going out to work and fathers being away at the Front and Sundays lost so completely in necessary chores that it was obvious that neither mothers nor Sabbaths nor family discipline would ever be the same again. No longer corrected for every slight misdemeanour, children began to taste, very carefully at first, the sweet taste of freedom.

Then, too, was the conscience that arises in times of war and other catastrophes that seeks to wrest from disaster the promise of future good. That their children might not suffer was an unspoken but generally accepted prayer of those in battle. In the rejoicing for deliverance and return to family life the aftermath of the war provided pupils with considerable advances in freedom and status.

My own schooldays began as the First World War came to an end: my memories of the signs of hostilities are only few and those uncertain. I do remember – I think – a fleet of German taubes (curved wing monoplanes) making their way silently overhead and odd things like the sound and commotion of gun carriages passing in the road and horses with lean haunches and mules with pointing ears; things like cap badges and khaki uniforms with the endless rough bandages that were called puttees. Certainly I can remember the sense of calamity on the day that a telegram arrived to say that my eldest brother had been killed in action.

Most clearly of all I remember a night when I was taken from bed to look out of the window and see in the black sky the immense sagging inferno of an airship drifting on fire. In the darkness there were people shouting as it dropped helplessly lower. It was about to sink, it seemed, just beyond our back garden but in fact came to earth a few miles away. Many other children, I have since learned, had a similar experience and always with the same parental motive. It was something, they thought, that we should never see again and it seemed worth waking us in the middle of the night to see the very shape and horror of violence and to hear the shaky cheers of frightened people because in the heroes' peace that was coming there would be no more danger ever again from the air.

There are a few other wisps of recollections of those years. Of familiar neighbours suddenly appearing in new uniforms with bright brass buttons, the fragile but priceless ration cards – and the songs. These could be heard being sung by troops marching by or learned from older brothers and we marched up and down the garden path with a stick on the shoulder for a rifle and sang 'Keep the Home Fires Burning' and 'Mademoiselle from Armentieres' and the funny one about Charlie Chaplin and the Dardenelles.

How unfunny the Dardenelles really was, of course, I had no way of knowing. Soon enough – too soon for my liking – the time came for me to go to school. A warren of an infants' school absorbed long days that sometimes seemed would never end. At eight years of age one then moved to the 'Big' school, a National and formerly church school that stood on the edge of the small town. It is there still, thatched and squat-looking, agedly supported by a spread of more modern buildings but still the same. Like a poor relative, it faces the sweeping grounds and magnificent façade of a prominent public school.

At each end of the school heavy iron gates allowed boys and girls separately into the high-fenced pounds we called playgrounds and thence into school. When the teacher appeared, shaking the all-too-familiar handbell, the pupils hurriedly formed lines, each line a class, and we had to shuffle our feet and find the right distance by placing our hands on the shoulders of the boy in front. All this was done with suitable gravity for the way of soldiers was still close to us and if we ever began to forget we were quickly reminded by the particular teacher who did this duty and who had served as a sergeant in the war. So we right-dressed and shuffled again, then turned on heel and toe in best military fashion to march in. 'LEFT ... LEFT ... LEFT RIGHT LEFT ...' The piercing eye of the teacher kept us in line until we entered the porch, where military standards disintegrated into a mêlée of bodies grabbing pegs for their hats, though many boys in fact carried their hats into the classroom hidden to some extent under a jersey or in a pocket.

When you went 'up' to the Blue school from the infants, the immediate difference was in the smell. This was not a world of plasticine and slates but of ink and chalk, dry furniture and rubbers. Inkwells, especially, with the pens and nibs and the paraphernalia of writing with ink, were to become important. There was the filling of inkwells – and the spilling – the stuffing of other people's inkwells with scraps of blotting paper, the illicit exchange of dirty and empty inkwells for nice clean full ones, and the scrapings and scratching as you dug the nib into the well for the hundredth time. So far as I can remember, nibs were nearly always crossed, for reasons hardly ever associated with the legitimate use of the pen, and when they plumbed the depths of the inkwell they brought forth a trail of viscous silt with which to make a dispirited and blotchy display in the English or arithmetic exercise book.

In some of the classrooms, dark and battered with age and loveless use, stood long old desks which may well have served the very first scholars. They were composed of thick timber on cast-iron, so heavy that they were only moved by the extreme demands of a school concert or the Empire Day tableaux. Five or six children sat uncomfortably on the backless form attached to each desk. The only relief to be obtained from a slumped position was to lean forward with the elbows on the desk but this was forbidden by some teachers and shown as an example of civilian decadence by the ex-sergeant, who made the point with the aid of a short, twangy, military cane.

However, arriving gradually were the new dual desks, the first expression in terms of furniture of the rising status of the schoolchild. They were still very heavy and static by modern standards, with fixed hinged seats that, thankfully, had a bar to support the back. These desks had fixed tops with a groove for pens and a shelf underneath. Unfortunately, any commerce with books and belongings on this shelf had to be purely tactual since it was anatomically impossible even for small boys to see underneath save by crouching on the floor. The location on the shelf of required books and pen was a problem and there was a frequent though punishable falling of objects on the floor. To solve this, cotton bags were made which could be tied by tapes to form handy envelope shapes and in these the belongings could be stored. They were kept on the shelf and drawn out when something was required. I remember how the bags were collected and stacked in the cupboard some time during Friday afternoons, and what a welcome chore that was, as it meant that for the remaining hour there would be no scratchng with our inky pens but a pleasant session with the 'silent readers'.

These 'silent readers' were a collection of two or three dozen single copies of the usual school classics, very short and abridged, and they came up dusty and brown and undistinguished from the depths of the cupboard on this weekly occasion. They were the sole books auxiliary to the 'lesson books' and were given out only as a treat – a concession to the new liberalisation of school life. It was little enough compared with the libraries of handsome books in schools today but a significant advance from the Bibles-only of the early years. They provided me with some of the happiest hours of my young life.

In this school the teachers' desks were high, with a tall chair from which the class could be viewed at a suitable elevation. Prominent on the desk was the short cane which in fact was not too often used for outright castigation but more often as a pointer, a prodder, a mover of elbows and a rapper of dirty fingers. On the desk too was the red pen and red inkwell used so awesomely for the register and the marking of books. A sum which had been correctly worked out in an exercise book carried not a humble tick but a large and triumphant capital R in red – a mark of distinction that I greatly envied but seldom, I am afraid, achieved.

On the wall were the unexciting series of maps that show the snaky black lines of isotherms on a blue background or dark brown mountains in a light-brown world. A row of pupils' drawings would be pinned underneath them. The cupboards were dark and massive, obstructive of light and space and though not fixed, they were seldom moved. Window pole, coal scuttles, a football and a broom kept company in the corner. Beside them was the fireplace, surrounded by a tall fireguard. On cold mornings teachers were fond of sitting on or leaning against the fireguard, thus claiming much of the warmth intended, in faith and hope perhaps, to be shed over the whole of the classroom. Even to sit down on the cold forms on a frosty morning was a chastening experience and the picking up and using of a pen at a desk well away from the fire was a tedious and miserable business. This was particularly so for such as myself, for whom figures had no magic or even attractive properties, for regularly each morning after Scripture we were bound to be doing sums.

However, in this and many other matters in our small country school there was a saving grace of interest and change due to a particularly enlightened and forward-looking headmaster. Perhaps envisaging the freedom that school life would enjoy in the future, he saw the system then as already out of date and accelerated the changes that rigid attitudes made so slow. The traditional antagonism of teacher and pupil continuing long after the payment-by-results system he was concerned to break and as far as possible to introduce the concept which is theoretically the basis of schoolwork today – of working together for a common cause.

His first overtures in this direction were met with the utmost suspicion. After all, he was a foreigner from another county and bound to be somewhat barmy by our standards. When we found that on cold mornings he did not sit on the fireguard but moved it away and rearranged the desks so as to make the best use of the fire, we were glad of the warmth but wary of being caught out by some schoolteacher cleverness. On such another morning when we were scratching in our exercise books with pens we could scarcely hold in our cold fingers, he looked round the class for a minute and told us to put our pens down. The next moment he had a tennis ball in his hand and was shouting 'Catch' to a boy peaked-looking and snivelling in the back row. At first, unsure of such unusual goings-on, the boy lamely and almost apologetically tossed it back.

'Quicker and harder', the headmaster shouted. Soon the boys caught on, the game of tossing the ball to each other became fast and furious and in a few minutes we were not only several degrees warmer but a good deal more cheerful. In those days it took a pioneering character to introduce such levity into the classroom and this he undoubtedly was. New books were brought into the school and new ideas; pens scratched away far less and the desk was sometimes abandoned for excursions out of doors. Even the timetable became something less than the immutable law of the Medes and Persians; English, with its endless exercises in parsing and punctuation, was turned into a challenge to write a story. Gradually we lost our suspicion and in turn made our own concessions, emerging into a much more open and enthusiastic relationship with our mentors than we had ever thought possible. In time even the least co-operative among us found occasion to be thankful for the new order of mutual help. The old seesaw of misdemeanour and punishment was somehow held in a much more reasonable balance and to some of us came the wild thought that we might even get to like school.

Even art could be endured, we discovered. Not that 'Art' existed in our timetable. The word would have seemed a social impertinence if used by elementary schools; what we had was 'Drawing'. Drawing itself was a considerable concession to new-fangled ideas that many people could accept only with the most dismal of forebodings. By compromise, drawing was held to be a suitable subject for the timetable only if it were allied to painstaking skill and usefulness, and nothing to do with ideas or expression. So we had drawing according to uniform standards. A piece of plain paper and an HB pencil were all that was allowed and

a popular object to draw was a vase or some other symmetrical shape, or a twig or an apple. Time after time we dealt earnestly with the task of balancing the opposing curves of a jug or convexes of a cup and saucer, using our rubbers in increasing pessimism of ever drawing the line in the right place.

Too often twigs turned out looking like heavy clubs which had sprouted leaves, vases wilted on one side or the other and an apple had the stodgy, unfruitful look of a ball of wool. Still we rubbed, as the virgin white paper became submerged in a murky creation of oscillating lines fringed with fingermarks and small drifts of rubber flecks would build up around our elbows as we sprawled on our desks in an agony of intense application.

Now at last we could leave some of this drudgery behind. Coloured paper and pastels were provided and a new conception of art which we had the greatest difficulty in accepting was repeatedly explained and demonstrated. The certainty that a pencil outline in the right place automatically encloses what the shape obviously represents is a difficult one to lose. By long tradition an apple was the curved line showing the outer edge; if the shape was right then the inside was naturally an apple. Now we had to bother more about the enclosed spaces and less about the lines. Lessons tended to become well-meaning chaos for a time, with confusion and doubt being covered with a sanguine riot of colour. Autumn leaves and ripe apples were bursting out on paper, on our desks, faces and hands. Although many of those who had drawn apples in pencil went no further than to draw apples in crayon, there were some timid efforts at landscapes and even figures. For most of us the only difference was that fingermarks were no longer black but coloured.

Using pastels was as far as we were allowed to go in the frivolous pursuit of art, so far as school provisions were concerned, though a few were encouraged enough to bring their own paint-boxes. But more drastic – and much more satisfying – than the discarding of the HB pencil was the consignment of the tonic sol-fa chart to the back of the cupboard. For years the chart had dominated our singing lessons, the teacher's pointer darting from Doh to Me and Soh to Lah (and always catching us out with the crafty half-note Te) in an unmelodious exercise that preceded the learning of a new song. Instead, to our astonishment and delight, we were plunged headlong into rehearsals for an operetta – so successfully that the only concert hall in the town was hired and for two evenings we sang our hearts out to packed houses. The profits bought some fine blue jerseys for the football team, a mark of distinction ahead of other schools in the area and another fillip to our growing confidence.

If the headmaster hoped, however, that by doing so he was weaning us away from our customary drill into the realm of games, then this must have been one of his disappointments.

The teacher-who-had-been-a-sergeant was unwilling to yield an inch in the matter of physical jerks and we continued to assemble for this rigorous routine in the playground at least three times a week. A basic part of drill, apparently, was deep breathing and we inhaled and exhaled to order until we choked on the cold morning air. There was a military flavour to the exercises which seems a little absurd in these days but was almost inevitable at that time with the consciousness of the First World War still close to people's minds. We marched and marked time, right-wheeled and about-turned and at the end of each exercise we stood at attention or at ease. With 'arms bend – stretch' we jerked our hands to our shoulders, then upwards, then outwards, then down. We touched our toes, ran on the spot, twisted our 'trunks', and I must confess, in the face of the hilarity that the thought of drill causes in many people, that we enjoyed it. There was some kind of pride then in the developing of straight shoulders and backs and these exercises gave me a sort of physical awareness that I cannot for the life of me think was a bad thing.

We continued with drill until the ex-sergeant teacher was wooed from his strict routines by the headmaster who slyly asked him to referee our school football matches. From then on he devoted himself to the new discipline of training us to win matches. By the end of the season we had won all our games and took the cup at a memorable final on the town's best football ground.

Such things are little enough in the achievements of schools today but in the twenties this was pioneering. So many innovations were made and fresh victories won as traditional attitudes gradually eased and scholars became pupils and school an endurable way of life. There was still a long way to go, however, before we could begin to dream of such things as equal opportunity in education or of further education for elementary schoolchildren. Nor had the time arrived to relinquish the time-honoured reverence for the gospel of keeping one's ordained place in society. Both the education that we obtained and the range of employments open to us were strictly limited. Girls still went into domestic service in the twenties, to the complete satisfaction of parents who remembered that in their day service in a large household provided a good and respectable life. Times were changing but slowly. Servants still abounded in the homes of the middle class and the rural gentry and only in the big cities were there young women who earned their living in offices.

As for boys, the more far-seeing parents had them indentured to a trade such as carpentry or bricklaying and although this meant several years' apprenticeship with only nominal wages, it was something held in almost religious esteem. For the rest, several would go to work on the farms which were still mainly horse-powered, or would take jobs as errand boys. The brightest boy of my last class at school became a telegraph boy and the envy of us all. Present-day criticism of such jobs as being dead-end or monotonous had little application in the twenties. In elementary schools we were destined for dead-end and monotonous jobs. We still, despite the First World War and advancing ideas, knew our places.

7

THE DECADE OF TRANSITION

THE usual reflection that the twenties were years of transition is difficult to resist. In so many aspects of daily life that decade showed itself to have been an obvious halfway house between the old century and the new. But the idea of transition is too mild for the twenties – after all, that is something that can be said about any decade – for times were not merely changing but in many ways a new age beginning. It was an original, a light-heartedly innovative period as well as a time for sloughing off old skins, when the word 'Emancipation' was used so commonly as to be a clarion cry.

It was a decade which not merely separated the Victorians from the 20th century but which deliberately set out to sweep away the cobwebs from the one and supply a new energy to the other. In the aftermath of the First World War a new reality seemed to seize the minds of people and all that represented the falseness of pre-war days became anathema. In 1920 it may have seemed likely that life would go on in the same old pattern but this was an impossible dream; by 1930 the domestic revolution had turned homes, fashions, habits and outlook almost upside down. Nothing would ever be the same again.

In the meantime, of course, there were the parallel changes brought by new inventions, particularly radio, mass-produced cars and rayon, but these did not really spearhead the new ideas. All was governed by the common impulse in people's minds. Time now to change and to rub clean the slate of the past. It was done literally and thoroughly, like some gigantic springclean that had been delayed too long. In what had been the fortress homes of the Victorians the new generation stripped the walls of the flowered paper, took down the blinds and the fretwork and beads. Only an ascetic simplicity would satisfy. Away with pictures and knick-knacks; have no more covering up, no more simpering curves or cloying artificiality. Bare the walls, bare the table, bare the room! If there is to be a pattern anywhere it must be in straight lines or in a 'cubist' design. Throw away the antimacassars and the aspidistras – already they are objects of derision.

Steadily, the domestic gods of pre-war days were overcome and the material objects that had been so much prized disappeared from view, at least in the homes of younger people, were stuffed into attics (to be rediscovered in more recent years as treasures!) or on to bonfires. The need to wipe the domestic slate clean became a compulsive part of life. There was a common desire to destroy all that was useless and ornamental, to invade the sanctity of the front parlour and show it as a room to be lived in, to open windows that had been cluttered with lace curtains, and front doors on other occasions than weddings and funerals; above all, to have clear space. The very features of home life that had been so dear to the previous generation had become impossible to live with.

In a similar calm but determined revolution, women wiped their hands of the past and presented themselves anew. Dowdy long skirts and petticoats were progressively reduced and then rejected together with the formidable styles of underwear formerly considered proper. Even the large-brimmed hat with its decorative hat-pins keeping it in place on the conventional 'bun' of hair was soon to go, as well as the veil, the laces and frills and the once-popular pieces of fur. The female ankle and calf were revealed and in about 1926 the knee was bared to wondering eyes for the first time. Almost literally, women had shaken off the past as it affected them personally and they emerged in a new, refreshing concept of feminine appearance.

Clothes were lighter, gayer – those of the 'flapper' incredibly slight, daring and frivolous – and the realisation that the old pre-war ways were dead and that a new, exciting period had begun was conveyed to all who cared to read by the Bright Young Things as they sparkled and shone in artificial silk and artificial pearls.

Reflectively, even men's clothes changed, with 'soft' collars replacing celluloidal neckwear, while flannel trousers (and their deviation into the extravagant style of Oxford bags) became almost universal wear with a blazer or sports coat. Plus-fours were an unmistakable status symbol and affected by many of the social-conscious males. Although it took many years before men began to consider relinquishing their hats, at least the cloth cap was giving way to trilbies and bowlers.

A young man going to meet his girl friend, which in those days meant that he was probably 'courting strong', might wear a shallow round hat popularly called a 'duck-pond', with Oxford bags and perhaps a double-breasted waistcoat.

Alternatively, a navy-blue, double-breasted suit was considered to be appropriate. A tasteful button-hole and a pair of patent leather gloves, one of them held in the other gloved hand, completed the outfit of the elegant young swain on a summer's Sunday afternoon.

Of course, all such innovations were introduced by the more forward-looking people of the twenties and they percolated but slowly through the layers of tradition and habit in country districts. The impact of the changing fashions was no more than a distant smoke signal in the wondering vision of the village school. Nevertheless, slowly the changes came – in dress, in ideas, in outlook, seeping through the strata from the Bright Young Things to the humble level of the cottage child. In the early twenties a boy could still be wearing the black stockings and knee breeches and Norfolk jacket familiar to the previous generation, with the hard collar, the heavy boots and cloth hat. By the end of the decade those in the van of school fashion would be wearing a woollen pullover, in summer without a jacket. These were variously called jerseys or guernseys – or 'ganseys' locally. They were buttoned at the neck and had colours banded on the turn-down collar. It became 'healthy' for boys to wear short trousers (though with the inevitable braces), and the short-trousers cult flourished until every schoolboy up to the age of 14, no matter how much oversize, customarily wore shorts, and the first long trousers came with the first job. I can remember now the prickly feel of the flannel on knees that had never been covered and the way the material seemed to drag at the legs.

With the first long trousers came also the first pair of shoes. It was a purchase so stylish, compared to the long-tried boots, that it seemed almost irresponsible, the more so in remembering the way that older people would scoff at such unnatural daintiness. But this was the country way, with its long-held priority for keeping feet and head dry and in their eyes a 'good' pair of boots was a heavy pair that came well over the ankles. Not only were such boots carefully chosen but they were accompanied throughout their long life by the important ministrations of repair. Most fathers kept a last and a piece or two of leather in the shed for the family's boots and they expected to cobble until the uppers gave way or, as I remember seeing them, with toe-caps giving way to reveal a gaping waste of yellowy straw. Metal plates were usually put on the point of heel and toe, with an assortment of blakeys and studs in between to reduce the wear on the leather. Three brothers who went to school with me had their boots mended with pieces of rubber tyre, thick and rounded. Perhaps they were heavy-footed boys anyway but I always recall them as using their unsteady feet as if they were deep-sea divers.

Reverence for boots was equalled only by reverence for hats − or caps. Only 20 years before, people had believed the sun's rays to be harmful and destructive of female beauty and little girls from cottage homes had worn big straw hats for their protection. Now the belief was slipping away like so many other beliefs and big hats disappeared, though many kept to the idea that a head needed special protection. Sun-stroke, especially, was lying in wait for hatless ones in summer and sudden death anywhere was usually attributed to the sun by knowing villagers, no matter what any coroner might say. In winter no less than double-pneumonia was forecast for a rain-soaked head, and during most of the twenties a hat or cap remained an essential part of a boy's dress. So close a part of him was his cap that he usually stuffed it into his pocket on entering school and sat on it to make an uncomfortable cushion during lessons. It was used in the playground as an object to throw or to kick − provided it was someone else's hat − or as a stinging weapon of aggression. Out of school it could carry birds' eggs safely above the peak, until some joker slapped his hand down on your head, or it would be used to throw into the air at dusk to try to catch a darting bat.

Such treatment over the long life expected of a cap turned it into something threadbare and ugly to behold. First the peak would crumple and take the form of an inverted V, then the covering material would give way and the broken edge of the cardboard stiffening would protrude nakedly over the boy's eyes. No matter, there was no shame then over such details, and while the hat could still be worn it would be kept and fought for over and over again.

Among the poorer children at school it was still possible to see signs of raggedness, of patches and darns and of a general makeshift diversity in their clothes. Boys were sometimes bare at the elbow or collarless or had their shirt-tail appearing from a torn trouser seat. Corduroys which had already done duty for a father or older brother were cut down into short trousers and despite the rasping whistle that they made and their uncomfortable roughness, they carried the considered virtue that they were strong and would last.

We were, perhaps, a motley spectacle but no more, I believe, because of poverty than because life was more individualistic in the twenties and what we wore, though darned and patched, was reflective of a family's independence as well as of its means. The idea of universal styles and materials from universal chain stores was too far ahead even to dream about – though Woolworth's had opened up and was selling a number of very humble items for 'Nothing Over Sixpence'. We felt, with pride rather than resentment, that a family had to fight to secure its existence and that the freedom to do so was reward enough. As children, we were far from sorry for ourselves, nor was anyone sorry for us. In retrospect, I suppose we were poor but there was no poverty then because we yearned for nothing. Those who talk of the twenties simply as a period of poverty only reveal the mercenary taint of today's standards and miss the whole point of those carefree days. In fact, we were often drilled by our elders with the idea that we were fortunate to the extent of being pampered, compared to the standards of their own childhood.

My own father would look round at the crowded table in the kitchen where my brothers and I sat for our meals,

observe our appetites and obvious health with pride and could not resist sometimes a note of self-congratulation in his voice when he spoke, as if we were indeed delivered into a land of milk and honey.

'These boys,' he would say to my mother with a reminiscent shake of the head, 'these boys, they don't know anything.'

True enough, we knew nothing and could share in nothing that was past but we knew that the words recalled for our parents the cruel nursery of their childhood in the nineties when meals were scant and the shadow of the workhouse lay upon the table. By comparison we were indeed spoiled and pampered. There was always food enough; our beds were warm and comfortable enough to young bones; we did not have to spend long, weary days in scaring birds or in picking stones. We did not even have to go to church on Sundays, though I believe that this was a sore point between my father and my mother who seldom failed to attend. For a time we attended Sunday school intermittently, particularly in the weeks preceding the annual Treat to the seaside, but by the ripe old age of 12 or so we went only occasionally as company for Mother or because there was a pretty girl in the choir. The days of family church-going were over.

But I wonder how 'pampered' our childhood environment would appear to children of today. Perhaps my own was typical, happy and robust in a way that can never happen again. Just after the end of the First World War, when I was eight years old, my father used his war-time savings to buy a small field about a mile from where we lived. The field had been used by troops throughout the war and was desolate with the debris and rubbish of army life. At one end of the field was an army hut which had served as an indoor rifle range, so long that my father planned to split it into two halves, one to be turned into living quarters and the other half to be partitioned into sheds, pigsties and stable. I can only imagine now, since at that age I could only see the fun of the task, the immense difficulties of building single-handed a home for a large family too young to assist, and when that was done, of clearing the field of its thistles and surface rubbish, of ditching and draining and laying hedges, of making roadway and pond and then digging with spade and fork the whole of the two acres of heavy clay soil. I think I know now what made the whole thing not merely worth while but an exciting challenge, despite the lack of any kind of financial support, or because of it – it was the feeling of personal freedom.

As the winter came on, the last of our furniture was carried along the lanes on a handcart and placed in the bare new hut ennobled with its address as 'The Bungalow' but still hardly more than a shell and smelling of new-sawn timber and beaverboard. Last of all, the pigs were walked along to their new quarters and the whole family of us followed behind them, one with a crate of chickens on a wheelbarrow, another with a pail full of last-minute debris, others with food or armfuls of toys but all of us wondering what the future held in store.

By Christmas the domestic conditions were still such that our Christmas dinner — of a pair of pheasants shot almost outside our new back door — was cooked in a makeshift oven of biscuit tins rigged up by my older brothers in the open air. I believe that this was a year in which we did have snow for Christmas and the youngest of us filled saucepans and containers with it. I remember what a disappointing task it was since the virgin white produced such a little amount of dirty flat water. Neither then nor throughout the 15 years that we lived there was there a regular supply of water, and one of the minor but constant chores was to fetch water from wherever we were allowed to fill our buckets and tanks.

Stephen J. Govier

- 1995 -

For all the difficulties of these primitive conditions and the need to grow and sell crops as quickly as possible to sustain the family, I cannot remember anything of bitter struggle or anxiety. There was nothing, it seemed, which could not be solved by a cheerful application of hard work and commonsense. To my father, nurtured in the hard conditions of the old century, it was an opportunity to use both his strength and his astuteness, and if he had doubts, we never knew of them, nor did it seem that he ever made a mistake.

In no time at all – at least it seems so in my memory – the derelict field became fertile and flourishing and the bungalow as comfortable as was required in those days. We were all sons in the brood, and not over-concerned about the niceties of an elegant existence, though my mother fought a losing battle over this. For us, rural bumpkins as we were, it was a good life, perhaps the best that a boy could have. There were always things to do and places to explore; buildings with the smell of hay and of apples; animals to attend to and spend our affection on; trees of all sorts to climb and the ever-changing plenty of the market-garden to assure us that we had all that we needed from the world. Sitting in the fork of a tree with a supply of apples and a copy of the *Magnet* was very near to bliss we thought – and I think so still. Indeed, we were pampered. We had all that it needs for happiness and no more.

Our childish content in those days may have been assisted, too, by the fact that educational ambition had not yet become possible for ordinary working people. The states of man, education-wise, were still immutably separate. Either you went to a grammar school because your parents were middle class and could afford to pay the fees or you were on the other side of the pale and took life as it came. Such things did not worry us then. The world seemed naturally appor-tioned between the higher social classes and the collarless. It was only later, when I was turned out of school to work on the land at the age of 14, that I began to look more closely at this arbitrary division into educational haves and have-nots and found that the School Certificate and matriculation was an immutable barrier. At that time regulations were rigid and specific. No concessions could be made, either in the requirements of the various occupations and professions which all seemed to demand matriculation or in the fact that you were never likely to obtain matriculation unless you went to a grammar school.

The impasse for such as myself was complete. Nevertheless, in complete despair after working for several months as a 'backhouse' boy and gardener, I went to see my old headmaster and told him I intended to study for the School Certificate on my own. He had the grace not to smile but loaded me with books, though he must have known how unlikely that achievement would be for me. I was no scholar, though a voracious reader. For three years I struggled alone with the books at the end of the day's work but was able to pass in only two subjects, which was quite useless since the Certificate would only be granted for a pass in five or more.

After that, my wandering studies took me a devious route that sometimes touched the fringes of formal education by way of University Extension courses, workers' colleges and the like but generally merely satisfied my own need to discover and to express logically something of that scholarship denied to me. In all it took 20 years of consistent reading and frequent importuning before I was finally allowed to pass rather shakily through portals that are nowadays held open in welcome to all.

8

COURTING AND ENTERTAINMENTS

As time went on, my older brothers reached an apparently lunatic stage of life in which they not only accepted but actually welcomed the company of the other sex. To those of us still at school it was something incomprehensible and somehow disloyal. The whole idea of 'courting' and having 'young ladies' with their mimsy ways and giggling voices seemed destined to spoil all the good times we had had. It was especially galling to hear brothers in the early symptoms of the disease trying to speak as if they did not know the Suffolk dialect.

The syllable 'ing', for example, which we normally disdain to use since it seems affected, would be suddenly perpetrated at our own tea table with shameless abandon because of the presence of some flapper. Instead of 'hope'n' and 'keep'n' and 'shove'n' we now had something that sounded like a shop doorbell. 'HoPING' they said, 'keePING' and 'shoVING', as if they could ring their way into the girls' hearts.

Their 'young ladies' were nice enough, despite what we felt was a dire intrusion. They were more fluffy and feminine, with their soft pleated skirts and decorative whimsies, than girls nowadays. Fashion then, as now, accentuated only one part of the anatomy at a time and since this was the period in which the leg was discovered and glorified in artificial silk, the female upper half tended to be camouflaged as a sexless area. The stock pictures of the girls of the twenties show them wearing cloche hats over their newly-bobbed hair but this was essentially a 'dress' hat. What seems to be forgotten was the saucy beret. Of all the head coverings ever fashioned, the beret must be one of the simplest and most utilitarian.

Without imagination in the wearer it can be merely banal. Worn as it was – almost universally – by girls during the late twenties and early thirties, it was an item of mischief, a piece of feminine charm that could assume a hundred shapes and styles between those that tilted cheekily over the eye to those that hung by a miracle to the back of the head. All in all, it was the beret rather than the more formal cloche hat that suited the daring and provocative flapper.

The girls wore necklaces – though not often those excessive strings of beads seen in recreated pictures of the time – and they occupied themselves largely in their leisure hours by powdering their noses. A shiny nose, even a hint or a threat of the slightest chance of a shiny nose was the most dreadful blow to feminine self-esteem and anyone who dared to suggest that a nose was shiny could become an enemy for life.

Perhaps it is that I am now removed from spheres in which noses are powdered as they used to be; certainly I never see it done now with the anxiety and industry that it once required. Perhaps shiny noses are now 'in'.

Sometimes, with their ever-ready powder-puffs and their rayon knees, the girls would come to tea on Sunday afternoons or even, round about Christmas time, to a party. Parties were rare in our masculine household and because of it, memorable. Like so many aspects of the twenties, parties became a mixture of the old-fashioned and what we regarded as daringly new. The new part could be jazz or dance band records played on the portable gramophone for young couples to engage in foxtrot or waltz but in a family party for all ages, as they usually were, this was not a popular thing. More often the older ways prevailed. Friends who were musical brought their instruments and in the parties I remember there was a concertina – a favourite instrument among country people – a dulcimer and mandoline as well as a violin. A jews-harp or a mouth-organ or a set of spoons were sometimes interpolated by well-meaning exponents but received little encouragement since it was felt that they were showing off.

On the other hand, ladies would be persuaded to play the piano and sing, as they might have done a generation before, the delicately sad lines of the old songs. 'I'll wander down the vale, lad, the last long vale of tears' are the words that come back to me and the male guests would take up the theme and sing 'The Old Rustic Mill' and 'Till We Meet Again' and 'I Passed by Your Window'. My father's favourite was the song about a girl who was 'only a beautiful picture in a beautiful golden frame', but the one we young ones always liked to join in was the 'Ten, twenty, thirty, forty, fifty years ago' which came in a heartening crescendo in 'My Old Shako'.

Older people liked to hear recitations when delivered with

the right amount of dramatic verve. If this was missing they turned on poor old Freddie Cooper, an ancient neighbour, stirred him out of his pipe-smoking reveries and like an old, neglected machine he began to croak and whine his way into some long-remembered ballad. Where it came from and how it managed to survive no one knew, for like so many others, it lived only in the shaky memories of old men who slurred their voices down to indicate the sad parts and brought a triumphant emphasis to the inevitable moral at the end. When such songs had been sung, the younger people would wind up the gramophone again and as their elders withdrew into reminiscences about friends nearly forgotten and events that had once been important, would listen yet again to the Whispering Baritone singing 'My Blue Heaven'.

Then, at the end of it all, when the singing and the giggling and the hand-holding came to an end, people had to get home. There never seemed to be anything particularly difficult or troublesome about this. Legs were still regarded as a sound means of propelling the human body and a walk of a mile or two after a party was of no account. For older brothers and their girlfriends the walking home in the quiet of the starlight may well have been the nicest part of the evening. It was the emancipated young miss, the daring flapper who went home on the pillion of a young man's motor-bike.

For most people the likely means of transport on all ordinary occasions was the bicycle, the willing horse of the twenties. A schoolboy would be lucky indeed if he possessed one of his own and as a rule he learned to ride an adult's, mounting the saddle from some convenient bank and balancing with feet high above the pedals. The boy would push off down some gentle slope, wobbling at first from side to side but gaining speed and unbelievably balancing as he glided into the exciting new experience. At the bottom of the slope the satisfying momentum came gradually to an end and the front wheel was wobbled towards the bank for dismounting. Then he would have to walk the bicycle back to the top of the slope to start again. It was something that could be done then quite safely on a country road.

Time after time the bank would be climbed, the boy holding the handlebars while gingerly putting one leg over the saddle as if it were some spirited animal. Then, after a moment of imprinted experience in which the pattern of the front tyre, the hot, slippery feel of the handlebar grips and the piece of cow parsley caught in the spokes were all part of the excitement, once more there was the bliss of gliding away in a powerless motivation. It was an experience that provided a kind of wonder, in the context of those quiet roads, that is not likely to be known in these more dangerous times. For me it was a much freer, happier experience than driving a car.

When one could balance reasonably well, the next step was to ride crouched on one side of the bicycle with one leg stretched through the frame to reach the other pedal. In this way, one could propel, rather uncomfortably and breath-lessly, a bicycle much too big to ride in the ordinary way. When, eventually, a boy acquired a bicycle that he could call his own, it became an inseparable companion. The state of the tyres and brakes, the punctures, the sound of the bell and the amazing tricks that could be performed were matters of daily moment. No wonder that when he left school a bicycle was the first thing for which a boy saved, and it was the proudest moment of his young life when he owned the gleaming new machine.

It was on a borrowed bicycle too tall for me that, at the age of 13 or 14, I began 'courting'. On summer evenings I would manage to propel myself, one leg through the bicycle frame, to the edge of town in order to meet the girl who had captivated me at school. She was a bonny girl with a fringe of black hair above large brown eyes and with glistening jet plaits down her back. She came like an Eastern princess from one of the small houses and we used to stand near the lighted window of the fruit shop on the corner. Behind her gleaming dark head there was the colour of the merchandise in the window – pomegranates and apples spilling from their proper heaps and resting on the wilting vegetables in front – and scraps of advertisements in strips across the panes. On one occasion we set off together towards the cinema but the prospect of sitting in the stuffy darkness had no fascination for us and we dallied outside for a time looking at the bright lights and the posters. Then we wandered back to the familiar corner with the fruit shop and we laughed and talked there until it was time to go.

Even when the summer holidays came we met at the corner and she was light and dainty in slippers and a coloured dress. We always waited until the lights went up in the fruit shop late in the evening and that is how I remember her now, warm and shining and content against a background of red-gold pomegranates. But the summer passed and the time whisked us both away to other assignations and perhaps to other corners. We were growing up.

It was not only the bicycle that was opening up new territories for the experience-hungry twenties. In our own homes windows were opening on an extensive new world through the introduction of wireless, though it came too haltingly to seem a miracle, as some have called it. Prominent in the apparatus of listening in was the tall wireless pole. When soldiers were demobilised after the First World War they were astonished, it is said, to find that the country had sprouted a forest of bare poles. At the bottom of every garden, it seemed, stood a pole at least as high as a house. From it stretched the aerial wire that entered the house by the window frame and was connected to the small magic box that was a crystal set.

These first crystal sets held a piece of quartz like a small cube of sugar and the extraordinary procedure was to 'tickle' the quartz with the end of a thin spiral of wire called a 'cat's whisker'. Sometimes the contact had precious little effect but by extreme patience a thin and distant sound could be educed and conveyed to the ears by means of headphones. The miracle, we knew well enough, was to hear anything at all, coming as it was all the way from Chelmsford. Too often, when something did become audible, it would be drowned by the rustling of newspapers or of someone talking and there was a good deal of shushing and of freezing into intense attitudes as if at some imminent revelation.

It was not long, of course, before the crystal-set gave way to the wonders of the valve set. No more cat's whiskers and headphones but dials and batteries and horn-shaped amplifier. For a time the condition of the batteries and the regular recharging of accumulators became matters of importance as the stream of sound increased and began to become part of our lives. Soon these sets, too, became obsolete as all-mains types with built-in loudspeaker brought in modern radio. The forest of wireless poles soon disappeared and much of the excitement went with them. The twenties were becoming sophisticated and little was ever likely to surprise them again.

We soon became blasé enough indeed, we who were children, to reject the charms of 2LO on Saturday afternoons in favour of the greater excitement of the cinema. In little more than a decade the magic-lantern shows had developed into 'the pictures' and already Hollywood was creating such films as *Ben Hur* and *The Four Horsemen* that would stagger and bemuse our country minds. Besides the 'big picture' in those days there was usually an adventure serial, week-long awaited and wildly heralded on the screen by cheers and whistles. William S. Hart was one of the first film heroes that I remember. He was a Wild West adventurer who was fearless in adversity, merely narrowing his eyes when confronted by his enemies and their vile schemes. Despite the regularity with which he found himself in their power and always just as the weekly episode was coming to an end, he was a hard man to scare and continued to fight strongly for justice.

Houdini (himself) provided one such series showing spectacular escapes and there was also a strange and terrifying character called the Iron Man who was encased in a kind of home-made suit of armour and whose identity was a great mystery until the end. There was also a cowboy-and-Indian series, the name of which I forget, which had in it a faithful Indian named Thomas who proved his sterling worth each week until he was basely killed by double-crossing whites. I remember that in our Saturday night bath my brothers and I cried for Thomas and would not be comforted.

However, there were many good films of a lighter kind – full-length ones like Chaplin's *The Kid* had people flocking to the cinema – and for many years there was a regular weekly two-reel comedy. Some of these are shown nowadays as vintage performances of Buster Keaton, Harold Lloyd, Harold Langdon and Fatty Arbuckle. The frantic pace of some of these comedies was a considerable challenge to the pianist who sat below the screen with neck craned to watch the action. In our local cinema everyone knew the name of this musical virtuoso and would shout encouragement from time to time if his efforts seemed to be flagging. Generally, he was very good and leapt from moonlight romance to storms and desperate chases with the utmost celerity.

9

CHANGING PASTIMES

GOING to school in the twenties was a leisurely but ever interesting experience – but so, in fact, were all journeys, for it was our ingenuous belief then that it was at least as pleasant to travel as to arrive. We had not yet achieved the modern facility for disposing of journeys as mere passages of time and such phrases as 'a two-hour journey' for example had little meaning for us then. For one thing there was no transport save the railways, so exact and efficient that one could make calculations about the time of arrival, but apart from that we were not disposed to look at travelling from such a mundane point of view. A journey was as long as it took and life was not yet so geared to the idea of speed that one counted the amount of time before the adventure.

The first journey that I can remember was a Sunday trip to the seaside in a horse and trap. It was a fine sunny morning and the church bells were ringing and there was great excitement in the house. Outside the gate the hired pony was tethered and it pricked up sharp ears each time we ran out with baskets and rugs to put in the smartly-polished trap. I think there were about three children with Mother and Father on this particular excursion and very soon we were all aboard and jogging along at a steady trot, the rubber-tyred wheels spinning briskly in the soft gritty dust along the empty roads. When we came to a hill we all got out and we young ones followed close behind in case the trap went off without us. We watered the horse at a stream that actually crossed the road and the excitement at this was such that we stayed to paddle in the sharp-cold water and then to sit down for some refreshments. The pony was unharnessed and cropped the grass at the side while we explored a wood nearby and found bluebells. Then we took our leisurely way again; altogether the journey must have taken something like three hours. Nowadays, the same journey can easily be done in half an hour though there is very little satisfaction in it. It is simply 'a half-hour journey'.

On that occasion it was an experience to taste and remember. When, eventually, we reached the edge of the North Sea, the sight of the great expanse of water crowned our adventurous journey with triumph and we must have gazed like Cortés at the Pacific, as indeed, we may have thought it to be.

In the cool of the evening, with the pony rested and all of us tired and satisfied, we set off back along the lanes that led homewards. In a short time we younger ones began to doze and only woke occasionally to the calm, interminable 'clip-clop' of the pony's hoofs, but I can remember to the present day how the cool air came over the brow of the trap and I remember the pony's forward-pointing ears and the smell of the reins. It was a journey that could not be calculated in terms of time.

By the mid-twenties such excursions were becoming rare. Cars were increasing in number and improving in reliability. Moreover, there were other ways to travel, for enterprising cab-owners were giving up their horses and going in for charabancs. I don't know why, except that I am a product of the twenties, but the recollection of the charabanc and the brake always seems such a good deal happier and carefree than the modern coach or bus. They certainly opened up a gay new world of excursions and outings that had never been contemplated before. At the same time, the country motor buses began to appear, looking like trams that had lost their rails. Like trams they were only partly enclosed; the top deck was open and so were the stairs. It was a pleasant thing to mount to the top deck by the outside of a bus.

An uncle of mine, who had followed the cult of automobilism from its beginning used to tell us how, 20 years before, he had been heavily fined and severely castigated by a magistrate for coming round a corner without sounding his klaxon horn. He had been travelling at over 16 miles an hour and caused a horse that had been standing quietly in the road grazing at the hedge bank to bolt through the village. Only a hurried retreat by my uncle prevented an unpleasant encounter with the gathering villagers, who were in a mood to set upon the reckless stranger and his noisy machine.

But the time was past for such scenes as this. Already we had the snub-nosed Morris Cowleys and Oxfords, which were considered to be very smart and progressive, as well as the hardy, mass-produced tin-lizzies and such familiar names as the Chevrolet and the noisy Trojan. Both the mechanics and the tactics of driving were still primitive and there was nothing very unusual about having a breakdown and reverting to Shanks pony. The only rules one had to remember in driving were to keep to the left and to keep a look-out when

Stephen. J. Govier -1995.

going out of a lane on to a main road. There were neither signs nor rules, driving test nor Highway Code. We learned, often enough, simply by trial and error; instruction was considered to be superfluous. It was easy to discover which gears carried you forward and the rest was left to experience.

Perhaps there was still a good deal of contempt for the metal contraptions by country people who had been brought up to use and care for the horse. I think we had less consideration for paint and polish than nowadays and when we had perhaps completed a journey minus a tyre or with a steaming radiator or at the end of a tow-rope it was never regarded as something calamitous but simply as proof of the perverse, undependable nature of mechanical things.

So far as the roads were concerned, we who went to school at that time could enjoy the best of the past as well as some of the excitement of the future. We could still, in fact, play our way to school instead of just travelling there as required by the conditions of today. At the beginning of the twenties bowling a hoop was popular. With a 'proper' hoop (not one taken from a barrel) and a handle with a curved hook at the end, running the road and pavement was a skilled and absorbing way of covering a distance, though carters and horsemen generally disliked the practice and made their feelings clear if a hoop came too near them. What with this and the noisy, interfering motor-car, hoops soon became things to play with only on your own garden path.

So, too, died out the whip and top. The small wooden halfpenny top had been a favourite possession of boys clever enough to make and wield a whip. They would crayon the top with rings of colour for the pleasure of seeing them whirl around, and having set them spinning outside their garden gate would contrive to keep them spinning, with some mad chasing and slashing with the whip, all the way to school. Such experts, like those who were adept at playing marbles or shooting pop-guns, were a select and dedicated few. For lesser mortals the whip would never strike the top, or if it did, would suddenly lift it over a hedge into someone's garden or greenhouse.

A favourite way of getting to and from school was to kick a ball along the road. The ball, once tennis and respectable, would be long shorn of its nap and without pretence at being anything but mud-brown. When the school gate was reached, after invigorating scuffles all along the road, the ball would be stuffed into the pocket, mud and all, to join the marbles and cigarette cards that were an essential part of school-going. There were many ways of playing football and moving along at the same time, though occasionally it did take an excessively long time. When we were already late and the sound of the bell was imminent, we would use the running-and-passing system which got us along pretty fast but on the way home, when there was nothing but a few easily-forgotten chores to interrupt our leisure, we had a full game with several players and goalkeepers who slowly moved the game along when they remembered. If a vehicle did come along as we played, it would at that time be by almost equal chance a horse-drawn or motor-driven interruption. Since we still had more respect for the horse, there would be cries of 'Hold the ball' before the cart or trap came within range.

If the horse happened to be that which pulled the oilman's van, the ball would be pocketed and the game abandoned forthwith, for the oil-van was recognised as an interesting if not always comfortable way to get home. The thing was to run behind the van, hopeful that you were out of sight, grab the top of the tailboard and clinging on to this with your hands, swing your feet underneath to rest on the back axle. As you did so the whole array of smells from the interior of the van would meet you, of paraffin oil and soap, candles, vinegar and polish. Any boys who could not find room to hold on would run alongside yelling: 'Whip behind'. The oilman had a soft spot for boys and usually took no notice, though the poor tired horse must have felt the extra load; but the basket-maker who never seemed to sell enough baskets to make him pleased, would flick his long whip round to the back of the cart if we tried it with him, and the painful sting on your wrists was a sharp enough warning to get off.

Rarely did we have the startling experience of seeing a runaway horse, perhaps trailing a shaft or broken harness behind it, a sight immediately frightening and sad. On one occasion, when some of us were trying to jump over a rope stretched across the road, the wild gallop of an approaching horse made us hastily loosen the rope and retire, to witness from the bank the unseeing panic of our neighbour's pony still pulling a small cart that flew wildly from side to side. A small boy clung in terror to the trail, sobbing and gasping at the violent pace and we saw our neighbour running towards us from along the lane as if there were any chance of catching up. Yet the old man followed, staggering past us with a look on his face that suggested the most pessimistic fears.

As it happened, the pony seemed to realise that it could not negotiate the bend further along the lane and careered instead through an open gate to a field, there losing its panic and its energy in the heavy going, and by a miracle neither horse nor boy suffered anything more than severe fright. It was not always so. Too often the stricken creatures would rush on to their own destruction no matter who tried to stop them.

Games did not always require to be played in the road; marbles, for example, rolled the better on the ashphalt surface of the playground or on the well-rolled paths that would later become pavements. At that time marbles were of coloured clay which could be easily crushed underfoot but were cheap enough at 20 for a penny to be grudgingly considered expendable. The alleys which were used for shooting were much more prized and very handsome with whorls of bright colours in the glass, while almost legendary in their reputed powers were the rare 'blood alleys' of stone or heavy opaque glass with a quirk of red in the vein. These never failed, or if they did, there was a good reason for it.

If a boy was without an alley, he could always break open a ginger-beer bottle and take the glass ball from the neck where it was used as some sort of valve, but such substitutes never seemed to have the power of the true alleys and were given the contemptuous regard they deserved.

The alleys were used strictly for 'shooting' and were not at stake as were the clay marbles. In fact, a boy would keep his favourite winning alley all through the season. The games were set out extensively over the playground and nearby footpaths and at this stage of marble history had no resemblance to the type of game played 20 years before. The name given to our kind of marbles was probably a local one and comprised the number of marbles one was prepared to put down, together with the phrase 'and a bit'. For example, 'three and a bit' or even 'four and a bit' could be suggested

but for practical as well as economic reasons we nearly always agreed on 'two and a bit'.

For this, each boy – usually of two or three – would place two marbles on the ground about two feet apart. Each pair of marbles would be several feet ahead or behind the other pairs. The players would retire to a line some four yards away and then, probably after some initial disagreement over who first had said 'First go', would bowl their alleys towards the marbles. He who was closest (and this

101

frequently brought into use the hand span in order to prove claim) had the right to play next. To excited protagonists the hand span could, of course, become a fairly elastic measurement and a good deal of derisive checking and counter-checking was sometimes necessary before the game could continue.

From this point the boy did not bowl his alley, but 'shot' it. This was done most dexterously by a trick of the fingers which I have never seen done since but was then practised with an extraordinary speed and accuracy.

The alley was held against the thumbnail in the crook of the first finger. It was a position which not only gave young fingers a deft control of the alley but with the pressure of thumb against finger there was a sudden release that provided a devastating catapult effect. Expert players, usually the more scruffy boys who spent hours kneeling and crouching on the hard ground and who hoarded their winnings like misers, could shoot with a deadly, chilling accuracy, knocking out marble after marble in a vicious massacre. After each shot they left their shooting alley ominously close to the next victim and the outcome of such games was only too familiar to novices like myself.

Compared with the incisive skill of this kind of shooting, the bowling of marbles, as played in the forties and fifties, was considered to be slow and ineffectual, although it was sometimes used as another method of playing along the road to school, when two boys would bowl their alleys along the gutter alternately in the hope of scoring a hit on the other.

When, for some reason or for no reason at all, the marble season came to an end, it was a good time to bring out our collections of cigarette cards. With these, while they were still fairly clean and flat, the first enthusiasm was to make up a complete set which could be as many as 50. Swapping and bartering gave the corners of the playground the excitement and perhaps the disillusionment of cheap-jack stalls. Most wanted were the 'Cries of London', 'Sights of London', 'Famous Footballers' and 'Regimental Badges', though there were many others that I have forgotten. The achievement of completing a set, however, was inadequate for those who were not of the collecting kind and very soon games were started. The most popular of these was for two or three boys with a miscellaneous stock of cards to drop one in turn from a spot on the playground wall about four feet from the ground. He whose card fluttered down to cover or partly cover another was the winner of the bottom card. Most boys carried a good number of cards loose in their pockets for there was something fascinating in the merely physical nature of a cigarette card. It was just the right size and the right rigidity to be nice to handle. It was smooth and coloured and there was something virtuous, too, in the fact that it was printed with information that one could read as a last resort.

What else did we have in our bursting pockets in those days? Knives, very often, though they had none of the sinister implications associated with knives in these days. They were usually of the heavy Boy Scout type and really more cumbersome than useful. There would be some string, the familiar frayed tennis ball, and probably an illicit catapult. These we made from a crotch of hazel wood with a supple sling cut from the tongue of an old boot attached to strips of elastic. With these essentials to carry around there was little room for objects like handkerchiefs, pens or pencils. If you came across a boy with a ruler in his pocket you could be sure that the only measurements he was likely to be engaged in was the distance and velocity that a tight little well-chewed wad of paper might take in a hasty flick behind the teacher's back.

At about the time acorns began to fall, we also armed ourselves with pop-guns. These had no relation to modern, shop bought ideas but required quite a bit of skill and patience to make. A short length of elder about two inches in diameter was taken from some convenient clump and the pith was removed, a good straight bore being finally achieved usually with the aid of a poker heated in the fire. Then a hazel stick would be whittled down with our huge and very blunt knives until it closely fitted the inside of the pop-gun barrel, leaving a short handle at the end. It was then necessary to make a brush at the end of the stick introduced to the gun, using our knives again to cut a little way down the length of the wood time after time until the fibres of the wood were separated. With patience and a good deal of spittle this came to form a brush which was able to force and keep air in the barrel.

The usual method of firing was to jam half an acorn in one end of the barrel and then to blow quickly into the other end while pushing in the brush end of the stick. Forcing the stick through the barrel took a bit of strength and sometimes the handle had to be banged against a wall, but eventually the point was reached when the compressed air would force the acorn out with a very satisfying loud pop and considerable velocity. But pop-guns, too, seemed to be really efficient only in the hands of experts. A small band of dedicated pop-gunners would devote themselves to the weapon with fearful achievements of stinging accuracy.

Many of the games and diversions that we knew have since disappeared in the wake of more sophisticated interests and organised activities. Surely we could not have lived together, the boys of the twenties and the boys of the present time. We would have laughed at the school uniform, the school books, the satchels, the carrying of pens and pencils, the prevailingly vertical posture, the clean knees and shoes; as boys now would laugh at the rough and ready, undisciplined country bumpkins that we were. The comparison is useless, for that time is gone and a completely new environment exists. Games and physical activities of infinite variety can be indulged in during schooltime at public expense; entertainment of the most luxurious kind is immediately available at home. Yet I would hesitate to believe that children are basically different in these days from children in any age. For us, our games and amusements were eminently enjoyable when we knew little else of enjoyment. A pop-gun is unlikely to survive in dramatic competition with filmed six-shooters on a coloured screen which can be watched in comfort.

However right and inevitable it was for us to have our hands perpetually dirty there is no doubt that such an environment would provide a cheerless contrast to a pupil's enjoyments in these days.

The impression that one's own childhood lay in a particularly golden period becomes deeply embedded in the passing of the years. When I think of the twenties I try to allow for the nostalgia that softens and telescopes the memory, making it seem that the sun was always shining or if it rained it was the warm, splashing rain of summer, and in winter the snow was white and unblemished and came in time for Christmas. Dinner was always waiting and always just the thing we wanted, dumplings and rabbit stew or suet pudding covered in syrup. The afternoons were timeless infinities. In the summer evenings we were called in for bed after the shadows came and we were tired of games.

Yet, even when I try to discount all the clouding sentiment associated with early recollections, there remain qualities which I think belonged to that decade – but never since – that existed in the sense of space and quietness and change, a kind of post-Victorian sunniness that by the thirties was already disappearing. At least we had the undoubted experience of seeing the old changing to the new to an extent that few other generations can have done. We were the last to see the farm waggon and the carrier's cart as prime users of the highway; skies that belonged only to the elements; the horse as the undemanding lord of the countryside. We lived in the last decade in which falling apples could wake a drowsy noon and in which at any hour you could stand, sit or play in the road.

Because we could hear and smell the countryside as it lived and breathed for miles around, the horizon of our senses was extended and the effect was to expand the spirit. In later years our senses have become restricted by the lordly machine to its own aggressive noise, to immediate danger, to days in which we cannot dream. The horizon has crowded in and the spirit rejoices no more.

10

POSTWAR HARDSHIPS

As, in these days, children travel to school largely by
bus and in the forties flocked along the lanes on local
authority bicycles – so, in the ingenuous twenties, we made
our way on foot. Not that there was any hardship in this.
The local school obligingly provided the modest learning
needs of the neighbourhood and travelling any distance to
school was almost unknown. A village kept its young to
itself, nourishing them in safe and familiar confines; from the
playground of the school many of them could look across the
green or the churchyard to their own homes. Even those from
outlying cottages seldom had more than a mile or so to
manage, which seemed little enough to parents who had
known what it was to walk long distances, and certainly not
so far as to prevent them going home for dinner at midday.

But though it was of little concern to us at the time, there already were influences designed to upset this cosy situation. The Hadow Committee was recommending that the whole system should be split in two and that there should be separate educational services and separate schools for those under, and those over, 11 years. No longer would children attend one school, moving from Standard One to Seven in simple progression but would be designated 'juniors' or 'seniors' and taught in establishments specially suited to the needs of the age group. The cry of 'Reorganisation' rang through the land.

It was no simple business to put such a scheme into effect. Provision of new buildings, transport, dinner facilities and new teaching concepts were expected to take some time. In fact 'reorganisation' went on until another war had come and gone and a new generation of children arrived who could not even remember the war. Village schools in agricultural areas were the last to be split and it was in the very rearguard of defeat that I continued to teach in such a school in 1961. I had no deep-based reasons for doing so but nevertheless while there was still an 'all-age' school I preferred to be in it. To me the atmosphere and the integrity of old country life was contained in the traditional village school and I was unwilling to see it go. In such a place, where one could hear the prayers and tables chanted to a lazy, almost musical rhythm that had been repeated over generations; where younger children were brought in and welcomed as to a clan or tribe; where the sound of the dialect and the ancient idiom fell naturally upon the ear – and where there was a continuity of loyalty and affection, it seemed to me that there was something here much more richly to be prized than the amenities of washbasins and sports equipment in a brand-new centralised school.

But that was a personal point of view and, I realised even then, probably a selfish and reactionary one. When at last the split came and the older boys and girls dispersed from the village with the air of lambs about to be slaughtered, their doubts and tears were short-lived. Having tasted and approved, they remained to enjoy all the varied offerings of a specialised school and to accept the opportunities it gave to extend and develop themselves. Their integration was speedy and their own enthusiasm for the exciting new life considerable; they had settled in. Within a few months they had learned to look, behave and talk like all the others.

It was in an 'unreorganised' school that I began to teach at the end of the war, though this was not a village but an 'Area' school. Perhaps 1947 was not the most inspiring time for a new teacher to begin. Like much else not immediately linked to the essential war-effort, the schools were obliged to mark time, making do with what they had and tackling problems as best they might until peace came. When it did there was the long lag of readjustment, during which the obvious thing seemed to follow the old pre-war methods and pre-war books. Although for many people the war had cleft their existence into two, leaving the past behind like the rejected half of an apple, in school no such cleavage occurred. Books were tattered and some unbelievably old; equipment was worn to the point of disintegration.

But even worse was the static, unexpectant atmosphere, as if war-weariness had settled like a cloud over the classroom. In fact, the seeds of change and revolution were already well and truly sown, but for a year or two at least, after the end of the war there was a cheerless welcome on the school doormat. For that matter it was cheerless everywhere you went – the end of hostilities brought little else except peace to anyone. It was obvious that there could be no sudden end to the privations and restrictions already endured through the war years and the prospect of life without ration-books, clothing coupons, and under-the-counter shopping seemed very remote. Optimism was double chilled, for 1947 brought a phenomenally cold winter and a peak in fuel rationing and power cuts.

One of the first school meals I ate was also the coldest. It was provided in a Nissen hut used as a dining-hall. The hut was unheated because of lack of fuel and due to a power cut there was no cooked food. Battling across the playground against the snow to partake of cold meat – the maligned Spam – and war-time salad that consisted of a great deal of raw cabbage was not the greatest encouragement to begin the afternoon's work. All, staff and children alike, sat in overcoats and scarves and left the cold jelly untouched and wondered if peace-time should not have something better for us than this.

In that long winter there were long weeks of unrelenting cold, with frost and blizzard, blizzard and frost, and the heaps of snow in the gutters remained so long that it became unrecognisable and ugly like blocks of cold, black stone. For those months and during the vast floods that followed, the problems of providing warmth and food were such as to put academic matters in second place in school priorities. There were schools which had struggled to keep open through all the difficulties of the war years that now had to close because they could get no more coke for heating. To those schools that were open came the immediate post-war children in their utility-branded navy-blue macs and wellingtons, children to whom peace as well as war must have seemed a dreary business. They had known the bleakness and discomfort of blacked-out homes and of air-raid shelters, of rubbery gas-masks and powdered egg; now, after the worst winter in human memory there was the wet and endless spring.

No wonder, when it was announced in a mood of mistimed generosity by the Ministry of Food that sweet rationing was to end, that a great tidal wave of humanity flooded into the sweet shops and stores and took away armfuls and bags full of the unbelievable plenty. Un-believable they were right to consider it. In a few days, despite the 'ample reserves' and the energetic measures taken to produce enough to stop the gap, the loaded counters steadily diminished. This fact alone caused people to buy more furiously, grasping what they could before it was too late. Suddenly the sweets had all disappeared: rationing was re-imposed. It was a very short glimpse of plenty and a very long time before people saw it again.

Children returned, as a matter of course, to the usual few ounces of liquorice allsorts, augmented in most families by the rations of older members who suddenly remembered that they did not really like sweets. Rationing had been so familiar to these children that they felt little hardship in the system. In their experience most things worth having were either rationed or 'in short supply', which meant either having something surreptitiously pushed across the shop counter to favoured customers or joining a queue in the hope that the supply would not be so short as to give out before your turn came.

Oranges and bananas, nuts and dried fruit arrived very occasionally in the shops and were only available at the head of a long queue. Even more prosaic things like saucepans, nylon stockings or alarm clocks had to be queued for and children learned to move along with their mothers in long crocodiles of expectant shoppers, many of whom had no idea of what was being offered at the other end. Certainly it would be something in 'short supply' and that was all that mattered.

At that time money was burning holes in pockets. Savings from hard work and long hours in munition factories and bounty at the end of completed war service gave people the means and the desire to buy goods which as yet did not exist. After the long lean years there was a yearning for luxuries and for acquisitions of all kinds. It was frustrating to be faced with empty shop windows when you had money to spend, or to be offered the shoddy or ersatz goods that had become acceptable in the urgency of all-out war effort. Even worse, perhaps, was to dream of food – not so much because of its shortage as its monotony – and to be informed once again by the Ministry of Food that there could be no concessions of any sort.

Usually, the Ministry would accompany such depressing communiques with pseudo-bright ideas for using dried egg, carrots or cod. For the first time, because there was now no clarion cry of war effort, such things became irksome. The restrictions and regulations that actually seemed to increase after the war, causing identity cards, ration books, coupons for this and that, permits for the other to be constantly required in daily life, put a kind of glumness into 1947 that had not previously been so noticeable. At this time even the supplies of beer, which had withstood the immense thirst of servicemen on leave all through the war, now dried up and local public houses opened for short periods at a time. Peace, it was said, had broken out.

It was inevitable that something of the atmosphere of shortages, of the ersatz and the utility should find its way into the schools in the early post-war years. It came in with the keen winds that blew in draughty classrooms, in the slush and rain that lay in the corridors all day without drying, in the bare, unpainted walls. But it did not come in with the children; there was nothing depressed or deprived about them. Whatever else had happened they had been nurtured on the best that was available and like my own contemporaries who spent their childhood during the First World War, they throve on the benefits of a conflict fought always with their welfare in mind. Gloom was only of the adult world and these confident youngsters refused to give it a second glance. As it happened, the bitter weather and the floods of 1947 suddenly resolved into a lush and beautiful summer. In the country we went out of doors, tasting the idea of holidays and relaxation, impatient for harvest; at school we went out time after time in the September sun to gather rosehips for syrup and blackberries for jam.

As the war receded and schools began to expand under the beneficences of peace and the 1944 Act, it became appropriate to extend our forages and to take groups on more distant trips and excursions. Many of them had never yet travelled very far from their own hearth and perhaps that is why any such visit, however seriously educational we insisted was the purpose, always took on the nature of a jolly good day out. In fact, it is a schoolboyish point of view that has lasted into these more sophisticated times that to travel on a coach automatically implies a kind of jollification. The belief is expressed in the amount of sweets, bottled and canned drinks and potato crisps disposed of on the journey and the apparent need to indulge in the singing of questionable songs. If the excursion is to a venue where refreshments are on sale, the day is likely to become a mere orgy of eating and drinking.

In this and many other ways a school journey is illuminating. Individuals of whom you thought you had the measure develop new and unexpected characteristics. Some children blossom, some fade; some are excited and some are sick. Generally, a somewhat more serious air attends travel by train. The links with familiarity are broken, the tradition of the jocular old brakes and charabancs bowling along the road is gone and a certain wariness creeps in. When it happened that a train journey was being taken for the first time, the trip became an exploration into new experience. It was possible, in the late forties and early fifties, to take a group of country children to London when scarcely one of them had ever been on a train or seen the metropolis.

The journey would begin in circumspect silence with a good deal of honest staring at fellow passengers and it would be some few blessed minutes before the children would realise that they were not imprisoned in a compartment (these were old-style trains, of course) but that there was a very convenient corridor that invited exploration and adventure. On every such journey the need to go to the toilet is insatiable; the discoveries of what they consider to be queer or dangerous characters are made further and further from the base. As the train enters London they stand and wave at everyone from the window but the impact of London, once they have disembarked, is subduing. Even the bright sparks find the whole thing a bit overwhelming to start with but joy bubbles to the surface again in Trafalgar Square among the pigeons and it is difficult to drag them away from the ponds in St James Park to look at more conventional sights. In the busier parts their astonishment is aroused by the escalators in the Underground, where they stand and stare in awe as human beings are carried down into the caverns below or up into the regions above. The pigeons and the escalators they will keep close in their memories to take home, almost forgetting St Pauls and Westminster Abbey.

Not all journeys were made so far afield. Often the school cycles were used to visit farms nearby. We would descend on the chosen farmyard in a swarm of interrogative humanity, like wolves, it seemed to me, on the fold. There we would wait for the farmer to appear and boys and farms being what they are, a closer acquaintance was immediate. In a few minutes we would be familiar with the contents and inmates of adjacent buildings, on friendly scratching terms with the sow and alive to the comic possibilities of Muscovy ducks. Despite a ban on excessive reconnaissance before the farmer came, boys would filter out of sight and send back messages by a lesser breed. In that way I would be able to learn that a Fresian bull had been located in the box at the end of the barn, that one boy had clouted another for pushing him over a bale of straw, that there was a nest of duck-eggs under the old chicken-hut in the paddock, that one boy had stuck his foot in a ditch or a drain and got it sopping wet and that you could climb any of the elms round the pond if someone gave you a 'bunk-up'.

The farmer appeared always far too quickly for these adventurers and the real visit began. Nevertheless, they would soberly gather round and take out their notebooks and pencils while the boy with the sopping foot would eventually stop making the hideous squelching noise with his shoe. The best part of the visit was over.

Our 'Area' school had been built during the thirties. Despite the economic difficulties at that time many such rural schools were set up and enjoyed a prestige that left far behind the standards of the twenties. The new schools were on extensive sites that contrasted strongly with the niggardly space of older schools and enjoyed open views of the country-side. In common with many others, our school was called a 'pavilion' type, consisting of a row of single-storey class-rooms and a central hall, each room giving directly on to an open corridor. Larger schools of the same kind were arranged in a square about a small quadrangle which unfortunately kept out the sun but not the cold winds that would funnel into the open space and blow ever cold along the corridors. For this reason many such cloisters have since been enclosed and spartan ideas modified to more comfortable conditions, but for me there was something pleasantly light and open-air about the old 'Area' schools.

Perhaps the most spectacular amenity of rural pre-war schools was the playing-field, with usually a reduction in the playground space, and in an expressive way this reflected the changing nature of children's activities. With organised games and athletics within the curriculum, the decline of playground games was inevitable. By the time the war was over, it was accepted – aided by the need to care for good school clothes – that games were something for which you changed into special kit and which took place on the soft turf of the playing field. The accompaniments of muddy knees and worn-out toe-caps of our games in the twenties applied no more. Physically and sartorially the schoolboy had moved up in the world.

To be sure, marbles were brought out periodically until several years after the war but in an emasculate kind of game that we would have scorned in my generation of players. It consisted of bowling an alley in turn to try to hole first in a scooped out hollow or in the hand-hold of a manhole cover and there seemed to be very little skill in playing. The appearance of marbles each year led me to investigate an idea that there was a kind of instinct among boys as to the advent of the season and that this was kept to a fairly constant date. After recording dates for some years I had to conclude that there was no rhyme or reason, certainly no regular date, for the marble season and that it began, like most children's games, by fortuitous chance. In any case, by about 1960 the game was to be seen no more in this particular neighbourhood.

Girls outlasted the boys in the playing of old-fashioned games and seemed for a time to be determined to continue their complicated routines with chants and skipping ropes and hopscotch. There were occasional sudden revivals of enthusiasm for certain singing games, circling and holding hands about some willing prisoner. In time, as children were drafted into bigger and bigger communities, these games, too, died out and it is some years now since I saw any of them being played.

With the ending of such games there came other changes. Together, they cause one to think that it was probably the decade of the fifties that brought the final transition from the early scholar to the pupil of the present day. Certainly his home life was developing in a spectacular way at this time. The wheels of peace-time industry had returned to full-time production and there was the happy domestic state of having money to spend and an increasing amount of luxury goods to buy. It was the period when many families bought their first television set, their first car, their first washing machine and perhaps enjoyed their first 'real' holiday.

In association with this material landslide is the evident growth of sophistication among school pupils and the relinquishment of their hold on the earthy grass-roots of their environment. What had once been a close, tactual identification with rural life became a rather academic interest in nature, in the same way that earlier participation in games of marbles turned now into a vicarious enthusiasm for games played by other people at a more professional level. No doubt the acquisitions at home and the rising standard of living generally helped, if they did not actually cause, the process of these changes. Television brought information and interest in zoology that was much more strange and exotic than that to be found in the local pond and the opportunity to travel far afield by car also tended to enlarge and make more impersonal the scope of the pupil's leisure interests.

Other influences too, came with changing times and changing ideals, not least of which was the prospect of an official examination for the secondary modern schools which would be comparable with those of grammar schools. The traditional 'second-class' rut was to be smoothed out into a common highway along which a pupil would be able to travel virtually as far as he wished. It was time, indeed, to carry a satchel of books rather than a pocket full of conkers.

11

TEACHING IN THE FIFTIES

Stephen T. Govier. 1993.

OUR school was situated deep in the heavy-land area of the county where corn inexorably changed places with sugarbeet and sugarbeet with corn and where the autumn days smelled of farmyard manure and ripe apples and waiting stubble. Children came at the 11-year-old stage from seven villages within a few miles radius and infants and juniors also attended from the immediate neighbourhood, making it an all-age school but top-heavy with senior children. Although there was a little tentative specialisation, in general the teacher and his assigned class were in day-long confrontation for the whole academic year, moving from the obligatory scripture period to the traditional early-morning arithmetic and thence to English. We all ate our dinners sitting at the same desks and brushed the crumbs away to tackle history or geography or some such matter in the afternoon.

My first class consisted of 40 children of 12 and 13 years old. They fitted exactly into the classrooms, in four rows of five dual desks — a heaven-sent package of young humanity in my apprentice eyes — and I believed, and still believe, that it was the nicest group in the world. If there had been a hundred such I would only have loved them the more. Perhaps it is a commentary on one's own failings, on dwindling enthusiasm and deadening senses, that classes tend to become less and less admirable with the passing years. Yet this is not entirely so. Some of the fault lies elsewhere, in changing attitudes generally towards cynical materialism which is inevitably reflected by the young and brought into the classroom. I feel thankful that I knew that charming mixed class of 1947 before the unaffectionate worldliness of later school life had touched them.

(At that time a group of pupils was still a 'Class'. It would have been a 'Standard' when I was at school and soon it was to become a 'Form' as the 1944 Act and the idea of parity of esteem caught up with us. In the same way, my old National school became an Elementary, then a Secondary Modern and now, of all things, a High School. It is part of the minor humbug of education to change names and hope that the nature of the thing will change with the label.)

To me then, scarcely having seen the inside of a classroom since I left the National school at 14, 20 years before, the boys and girls that I encountered seemed immensely advanced and liberated compared with those I remembered. There were none of the signs of poverty and neglect common in the twenties — boys were well cared for and neatly dressed and no longer weighed down by family chores, while the girls (in this my first school at least) were superior to the boys in their self-confidence and ability. In their attitudes, too, these children had advanced more in a generation than seemed possible. They came into school in the morning with the freshness of the countryside in their faces and as unworrying and friendly as they went out again at four, with only a few characters of the old type who were at all withdrawn and suspicious.

Obviously, these children were much more in concert with life around them than the scholars of my time had been and they had a much shrewder idea of values outside their immediate experience. The gulfs that had once isolated children from understanding and participating in the adult world were disappearing. In radio broadcasts alone a vast new world was being communicated to them in which the pattern and motives of the social system were becoming more comprehensive. Teacher, parsons, parents – all merely just people with failings who were trying to earn their living honestly, no longer sacrosanct and awe-inspiring.

There were other influences, of course, which allowed children to escape from the slough of the earlier part of the century, in particular the rising status of the farm worker. Certainly it was something of a revelation to me to see them emerge every morning from small cottages no longer earthy or cowed, but clean and charming. The girls stood straight and were as beautiful as desert flowers and obviously the heart of the family's pride. With their brothers they had no doubt but that the world would provide well for them.

As yet, in 1947, it was impossible to insist on a school uniform as something complete and unvariable, but a considerable degree of neat uniformity was achieved because of the good-looking standardised clothes that could now be obtained from large stores. Most girls managed a white blouse and a tie, with a grey pullover or cardigan. Even with the familiar Utility mark, the clothes were light and attractive. The signs of darning and make-do had all but gone and the unfortunate conglomerates of dress of my contemporaries were, happily, no more. Instead of lace-up boots or shoes, most girls wore low sandals, flat and comfortable, and the white ankle-socks that were very popular at that time. It gave them a fresh and youthful appearance which has long since been discarded in the wake of more sophisticated ideas. Underneath, they wore the almost universal navy-blue gym knickers and white vest and in this undress uniform they could be prevailed upon to perform their gymnastic exercises for the appropriate mistress.

Boys, just as kindly dealt with by the changing times, were able to wear low shoes with their suits, or jackets and trousers, which now tended to change from short to long at the momentous age of eleven. Never having known the agony of celluloid collars they generally appeared neatly collared and tied. Hats, except for the small school cap, had become rare though some boys clung to theirs out of respect for the journey they had to make by cycle to and from school.

For a time after the war the search for signs of physical neglect continued but the exercise had already become merely academic. A new breed, not only washed but enlightened, had arrived.

The fascination of dealing with my first group of pupils led me into excesses of zeal from which probably very little good came. Every child in the class was studied, card-indexed and recorded to the smallest detail. It was not enough to know IQs and 'Reading Ages' but whether they were 'Aggressive', for example, or 'Retiring'. I watched them at work and at play, picked out the 'Gregarious' and the 'Shy' and even followed them home to their villages on odd occasions to find out something about their 'Home Background'. Their position in the family, their brothers and sisters, pets and reading matter all accumulated in what was supposed to be a revealing picture of each child. I do not now think it was anything of the sort, for human nature is inclined to ignore labels and to object to being classified and all the data that I collected seemed to have had very little use. Perhaps I could give as an excuse for all my earnest efforts the fact that I was now doing for the first time the job for which I had spent half a lifetime trying to qualify and with children for whom I had admiration and affection. At least, I suppose, from it all I learnt something about myself.

I also collected some very good howlers:

'Sir Walter Raleigh was the first man to invent potatoes. He also had a bicycle named after him.'

'Cranmer refused to become a Catholic. Mary had him burned to a steak.'

'A Golden Wedding is when you have been married fifty times.'

History, unfortunately, not only reveals vast gaps in the memory but also a desire to fill the gaps with some kind of fuddled nonsense in the vague hope that it may miraculously turn out to be correct. To the history teacher who believes he has made all quite clear to his class the howlers that appear on the examination paper may not immediately appear to be excruciatingly funny.

Perhaps it was rather in spite of my researches that the members of the group came to unfold themselves to me as individuals. Among them were boys and girls who have reappeared in only slightly different guises at other schools and in other places during my teaching life. It is not so often the recurrence of physical similarities, though these can sometimes be surprising, as of a kind of personality.

One of the types I soon came to recognise, apart from the obvious rascal, the complete extrovert and the perennial animal-lover present in every class, was the persistently helpful character. Whether boy or girl, it is someone who constantly appears at your elbow like a genie when there is something to be done that is not learning. He is devoted, it seems, to the idea of service and the happy accomplishment of chores. He may, or may not be, as I discovered after some years, a 'leap-frogger'. If he is, he will serve you diligently until his ministrations bring him to the attention of someone higher in the school hierarchy whom he will then follow just as slavishly until his work comes to the attention of the headmaster. He cleans and tidies his way up a ladder as ruthlessly as the best. Once he has run messages for the Head he will not deign to tidy your cupboards again.

The jokester rears his head occasionally, asks permission to propound a riddle – usually at a most unsuitable moment – and divulges it between great shudders of laughter. The extraordinary thing is that they nearly always tell the oldest jokes and riddles, and even the ancient 'Why did the chicken cross the road?' turns up from time to time as if it were brand-new. The riddle-peddler is a menace because he will remind everyone else in the class of all the riddles they know.

More puzzling than these flamboyant characters are those few who exist in every class and appear to have neither vice nor virtue – who use passivity as a means to camouflage themselves almost to the point of invisibility. Assessing and reporting on these, even remembering them, is a difficult task and generally an assessment is made on the side of kindness rather than of truth in the hope that a little unexpected encouragement may strike some spark in their quiet natures and lead to better things.

In my original class of 1947 I came to have respect not only for many individuals but for the age-group as a whole. The years 12 to 14, scarcely out of childhood, is an age when, with more understanding and skill than we usually give them credit for, children look at life and form their conclusions with a bright, sane balance. Their judgment is perhaps the purest that can be obtained – a quality that cannot be compensated by experience. In only a year or two more they will be subject to the emotions and half-digested ideas of adolescence and after that to the influences of adult life where personal interests mar impartiality. Now, for a short time they have no axes to grind and their honesty is complete. It is usually because their conclusions are unflattering to adults that we discount their value.

But no doubt schoolboys have learned from their elders to be more devious nowadays. One thing they have not completely lost, though it tends to disappear sometimes, is the use of the word 'sir' when addressing a male teacher. After all, it is a monosyllable easy to say and which lends itself to a variety of intonations to the young expert. Without this convenient and undemanding label the teacher-pupil association becomes a bit more awkward and more so for the sir-ers than the be-sirred.

As a suffix, it is often used as a safety-catch to a piece of impudence, a cushion to soften an outrageous liberty. At all times it is a sop, a placebo with no meaning but nevertheless fills all sorts of situations, being both flattering but demanding, insistent but placatory, a tried and useful remedy for both the wide-eyed innocent and the world-weary old stager of 15.

From the ever-present young extrovert the epithet is a constant recall to his egoism and is heard as a repetitive hiss of a 'Sir' like some frantic serpent. The hiss is often accompanied by a series of karate-like chops of his hand through the air to ensure that, one way or another, you are not going to overlook him.

To the small, shy character it is a word to hide behind. 'Please sir,' she murmurs, '. . . sir.' Perhaps she never intends anyone to hear what she says. It is possible that she never says anything except 'rhubarb, rhubarb, sir.' Her achievement is to 'sir' her way into the general currency of the classroom and then to retire, apparently satisfied.

Sometimes the emphasis on the one syllable tends to exclude more important ones and this can lead to a breakdown of both patience and information. For example the question – 'Who wants to visit the gasworks next Saturday?' will probably elicit from the group something like: 'S'r, SIR, suh, S', S', SIR, N'Suh, Uh Suh.' To old ears it is impossible to sort out the eager would-be visitors from those who are declining and those who want to make the point that the gasworks is not really the place they had in mind for an excursion and a few who join in just for the fun of it. Perhaps the simplest way is to pass round a list on which they can write YES or NO without any sibilant overtones.

Yes, generally speaking, they are happy with 'sir'. They would be happier still if they could call every female teacher 'miss'. Unfortunately, feminine protocol creeps in here and greater care has to be taken to be inoffensive – or otherwise, of course.

It is not so easy to find a word for them. Perhaps because of sentimental connotations the word 'children' can be almost as embarrassing to say as 'God'. Many teachers will use the unpleasant term 'kids' but most will try to avoid both words by the impersonal 'them' and 'they'.

When school gatherings are addressed, the word 'children' sticks in the throats even of the visiting clergy. Clearly the raw material of modern schools cannot be compared with the children of Victorian novelists, ever cherubic and lisping except when bravely dying. It is easier just to refer to 'them'. Fortunately it is not yet 'Them'.

I think that the nearest they come to the cherubic is during the first week of the autumn term, the beginning of the school year. They are fresh, physically and mentally clean and braced to receive the onslaught of lessons, primed with a staggering array of new pens and equipment and a certain amount of admonition from parents and what is more, they have become thoroughly bored with the long holidays. For a few days, before good intentions are sunk in the hurly-burly of the term, the words of 'sir' are golden with wisdom. It will not be so again until the very end of the year when the same pupils are due to move. Then they will stand around with lugubrious faces, mutely indicating that it will do no less than break their hearts to move into some other form next term and, even in these hard days, there will be one or two who will anoint the parting with a tear.

The pattern does not change very much, though it does not often reach the high drama of an end-of-year farewell that I witnessed over 30 years ago. The much-loved headmaster was saying goodbye in front of the assembled school and before he could finish the whole crowd gave way to a sobbing and wailing in genuine lament that was loud enough to drown the end of his speech. Perhaps these were the last of the ingenuous ones – the sort of country schoolchildren that I have tried to recall and I hope I shall be forgiven for ending my short account at about the same time, the early fifties. It is a sign of my ageing prejudices that I look back at least that far for the sight of schooldays that were golden and children as yet untouched by the cynical attitudes of later years. Somehow, that kind of innocence seemed to go out of fashion at the same time as their ankle socks and their cotton dresses and their bicycles.

The bicycles were, of course, those provided by the local authority and at that time the school cycle sheds were full and overflowing with the black, utilitarian machines. Wherever they stood or leaned or fell over there were signs of hard usage in the loose battered mudguards, the saddles without springs and the pedal spindles that had no pedals. Here and there some string or wire contrived to keep the machine mobile but pumps and bells were rare and even the best of these unbeautiful wartime products brought little joy to the owner. Many pupils, nevertheless, had to travel five or six miles to their homes and in wintertime endured a good deal of grim weather. The capes and leggings that were officially provided kept out the rain to some extent but often there was a group of steaming children drying out by the radiator in the comparative privacy of the Head's room.

The cyclists used to arrive in the mornings in pairs or in village groups whose members hardly ever varied, converging on the school from the different country roads like staid and purposeful caravanserai. Perhaps it was the old-fashioned nature of some of the children that invested these cavalcades with the same solemnity that they used in saying their evening prayers.

'Lighten our darkness...' they said and put their hands together because pupils had always put their hands together and no one had yet told them not to. Their eyes were closed as they chanted in the peculiar way that each new child learned when it came into the school.

'Defend us from all the perils and dangers of this night. Amen. Goodnight, sir.' It was all part of the same recitation. There was a set response required which I only learned by trial and error and in intercepting a few embarrassed glances. When at last I had the wit to say simply: 'Goodnight boys and girls' I knew that it satisfied them. It was the ritual they knew and I had no wish to change it.

At the words they would file out and make their preparations for the homeward journey. While some of the boys disentangled their own machines with a clatter that forebode a further crop of loose mudguards on the morrow, the girls would deal with coats and gloves and satchels and then wait, one foot on the pedal in the tarmac driveway, for any laggard friends. When a group was complete it would push off quietly, closing up as the riders took to the road with the calm assurance of seasoned travellers to whom comfort and decorum were more fitting than childish excitement. Such behaviour was left to some of the local boys who, having but a short journey to make, could afford to show off and 'carve up' the girls as they went sedately along.

The general exodus from the school gate in the afternoon was always done, in those days, in the presence of the teacher on duty. Standing at the gate on periodic sentry-go was a chore that entailed very little effort for there was scarcely any traffic but allowed the opportunity to observe and even to give way to quiet contemplation. Since it was a duty with priority over all, the last bell of the afternoon brought one suddenly to the surface in the restless, crowded classroom to beat the stampede for the playground and the gate. There, before even the first of the children appeared, one had a few moments of contrasting calm. While the tensions of the classroom still sang in one's ears here was the unbelievable quiet of a bird sitting on the gatepost and a man placidly hoeing his garden.

But already the compulsive hurriers have appeared, racing like mad for the exit. They are the boys who, because of their nature, must be first out or die, figuratively, in the attempt.

Their energy is quickly spent in the empty road and they are not really far ahead when the little ones begin to sidle out of the gate and wait against the bank for older brother or sister. The boys who live nearby mount their bicycles and buck and shout in the cause of freedom while other boys on foot set about pulling them off in the cause of a levelling society. Flotillas of cycles assemble and drift away. Already the road is flooding with departing figures.

This is their road home. At the end of the day in school it is their route of escape. Perhaps, in years to come, it will be remembered when much of school life is forgotten. For everyone who has ever gone to school there has been a friendly and familiar road home – from those early scholars of the British and National Schools who trudged their dust-strewn lanes to those who nowadays sweep along smooth metal surfaces in the insulation of school buses. In the twenties, when our road home was still rough and all but empty, it was the mystic road of Masefield's 'The Seekers', for this we learned and sang in school.

'We travel the dusty road, till the light of the day grows dim,' we used to sing. 'And the sunset shows the spires away on the world's rim.'

And the gaslight would be soberly hissing in the afternoon gloom of the classroom as we concluded: 'For we go seeking cities that we shall never find.'

The words sift into my memory as I stand at the gate and watch the children go. Do they, walking and cycling the quiet roads to their homes, seek cities that they may never find? How can one tell? Out of the fret and toil of lessons, what do they really take home with them at the day's end and the term's end? Surely it is something more than facts – perhaps something from the atmosphere of school, for example, from the accumulation of activities or the varied relationships, or something merely in a word or a picture or a beam of light across the playground. Certainly it must be more than facts, more valuable than knowledge. Watching them go at the end of the day, the concerns of lessons dwindle into minor importance in recognition of a larger perspective, and it is courage and loyalty, rather than history and geography, that you hope they are carrying home with them.

Faces turn toward you as they go past. 'Goodnight,' you say, 'goodnight, goodbye.'

Goodbye all. Your faces are clear though I cannot tell if they are the faces I knew yesterday or last year or a score of years ago. The tide of fresh young faces comes in ever again, year after year; it is the teacher's elixir of life, perhaps the only kind of immortality. As I watch them disappear along the road, their country lives set sound and deep in the unpretentious earth, I am sure again that a teacher is given a special privilege.

But the time for contemplation is over. The road is empty and my gate duty performed. Behind me, the empty shell of the school still echoes and vibrates.